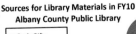

You: Losing Weight

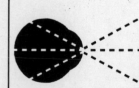

You: Losing Weight

THE OWNER'S MANUAL TO SIMPLE AND HEALTHY WEIGHT LOSS

Michael F. Roizen, MD
Mehmet C. Oz, MD

THORNDIKE PRESS

A part of Gale, Cengage Learning

GALE
CENGAGE Learning™

Detroit • New York • San Francisco • New Haven, Conn • Waterville, Maine • London

GALE
CENGAGE Learning™

Material in this work was excerpted from *YOU: On a Diet* (revised edition).
Thorndike Press, a part of Gale, Cengage Learning.

Thorndike Press® Large Print Health, Home & Learning.
The text of this Large Print edition is unabridged.
Other aspects of the book may vary from the original edition.
Set in 16 pt. Plantin.

LIBRARY OF CONGRESS CATALOGING-IN-PUBLICATION DATA

Roizen, Michael F.
    You, losing weight : the owner's manual to simple and healthy weight loss / by Michael F. Roizen, Mehmet C. Oz.
    — Large print ed.
        p. cm.
    Originally published: New York : Free Press, c2011.
    ISBN-13: 978-1-4104-3910-9 (hardcover)
    ISBN-10: 1-4104-3910-0 (hardcover)
    1. Weight loss. 2. Low-fat diet. 3. Reducing diets. 4. Large type books. I. Oz, Mehmet, 1960– II. Title.
    RM222.2.R6266 2011
    613.2'5—dc23
                                                2011019287

Published in 2011 by arrangement with Free Press, a division of Simon & Schuster, Inc.

Printed in the United States of America
1 2 3 4 5 6 7 15 14 13 12 11

To the millions who have dieted
hard, so they can learn to diet smart

THE YOU DOCS

Dear Readers,

If you're picking this up, then chances are that you — or someone very close to you — want to drop a few pounds, trim up, and change your body. And chances are that you've heard about every weight-loss strategy possible: your friend's favorite turnip-only diet, your neighbor's secret pills, a body cleansing that makes you think you feel like you've spent three days on the wrong end of a plumber's power tools. You've got a problem? Everybody has an answer.

Many people like to say that there are no shortcuts when it comes to weight loss — no magic bullets, no 20-pounds-in-3-days formulas, no way to get from size XXXL to size S by the end of the weekend. In a lot of ways, that's absolutely true. But here — in this exclusive excerpt from *YOU: On a Diet* — we want to offer you a form of a shortcut: The best 99 tips and strategies from our bestselling book that will help you get your body where you want. And for starters, how does 20 pounds in 6 weeks sound? Great? We thought so. And it's absolutely doable if you take the time to follow our main mantra: Diet Smart, Not Hard.

What's that mean? Our goal is for you to make changes in your life, but we want to make living healthy automatic, so you don't have to obsess over healthy living — and feel guilty when things go a little offtrack. The fact is, the more you can make smart choices an automatic part of your life (and not an hour-to-hour struggle), the better off your body (and mind) will be. This book will show you how.

In our book, *YOU: On a Diet,* we take you through all the biology of blubber. We teach you why your body works the way it does, because we believe that understanding those processes will help propel you into action. But we also know that sometimes, you just want to drop your fork, push away your plate, unbutton your pants button, and say, "Get to it, doc! Tell me what to do."

And that's what we're going to do

right here. We're going to get to it. We're going to give you the shorthand version with all the tips and insights to get you going and help you lose weight. We'll cover our overall philosophy, food, exercise, your mindset, your lifestyle, and more. And within these pages, we're confident that you'll have the informational ammunition you need to make changes in your life — so you can best enjoy life.

Here's to a healthy and happy YOU, Michael Roizen, M.D., and Mehmet Oz, M.D.

BODY BASICS

1. Know That Knowledge — Not Willpower — Is the Ultimate Weapon

Most dieters try to defeat their Oreo/ Cheez Doodle/custard pie infatuations with will, with deprivation, with sweat, with a "my-brain-is-stronger-than-your-crust" attitude. But trying to beat your body with mind power alone may be more painful than passing a melon-size kidney stone. Instead, you have to learn about the systems and actions that influence hunger, satiety, fat storing, and fat burning to fine-tune your corporeal vehicle so it runs on autopilot and takes you to your ultimate destination: a healthy, ideal body.

2. Appreciate the Biology (and Complexity) of the Body

One of the reasons why most so-called diets fail is because of a psychological and behavioral flaw that many dieters have. We desperately want to believe the simple, comforting promises that diets make — that doing A always gets us B. Because once we see that A (eating wheat germ 24–7) doesn't always equal B (the cover of *Vogue*), then we get frustrated and angry and give in to the gods of cream-filled baked goods. Unfortunately, your body and your fat do not have a linear two-step relationship. Instead, think of your body as an orchestra. All of its systems, organs, muscles, cells, fluids, hormones, and chemicals play different instruments, make different sounds (your intestines have dibs on first-chair tuba), and produce different results depending on how you use them. They work independently, but only when they're played together can you appreciate the magnificent symphony of your own biology. As the conductor of your biological orchestra, you control how the instruments interact and what the final result will be.

3. Let Your Body Guide Your Choices

While we want you to "not think" about eating good foods, we also know that "not thinking" may be how you got into this pants-stretching mess in the first place. When you don't think about the consequences of ordering football-size calzones, you wind up with such pleasantries as high LDL (lousy) cholesterol, low HDL (healthy type of) cholesterol, a fat-filled liver, inflammation in your arteries, and a higher risk of aging arteries that cause memory loss, heart disease, and even wrinkles, as well as a steady stream of coupon offers from the large men's department. We want your body to guide you to the *right* choices — without thinking about them — so that they'll lead to the results you want. It will take some effort at the start to retrain your habits, palate, and muscles, but this program will serve as a lifelong eating, activity, and behavior plan that will become as routine as going to the bathroom before bed.

4. Know It's About Waist, Not Weight

Some people haven't stepped on a scale since *Laverne & Shirley* played in prime time. And that's a good thing. For our purposes, you don't need to know how much you weigh (but if you want to check your progress on this program, then go ahead and peek). All you need is a tape measure. Measure the circumference of your waist at the point of your belly button (suck in; you will anyway), and record the score here. (Depending on how your weight is distributed, you may need to make an adjustment to where you place the tape. If you're overweight, keep the tape measure parallel to the floor during measurement.)

Your Size: _____

For optimum health, the ideal waist size for women is 32 1/2 inches; once you hit 37 inches, the dangers to your health increase. For men, the ideal is 35 inches, and the dangers to your health increase once you hit 40 inches. While we emphasize waist over weight, we also know that many of you won't be able to resist the siren of the scale. When it comes to actual weight, you do need to stop thinking about one specific number. ("I want to get down to 130.") All of us have an ideal playing weight — not a weight for running marathons or making All Pro linebacker or posing for an airbrushed-anyway centerfold. This ideal playing weight is a *range* in which you live lean and healthy, and one in which you significantly reduce the risks of aging diseases associated with being overweight.

5. Draft Your Team

You have to stop thinking that this game is you versus a stadium full of rib-loving opponents. Sure, you need to be the quarterback of your waist control team, but you won't achieve success without a team that can block for you, high-five you when you're doing well, and give you an encouraging smack on the butt when you're not. Your starting lineup should include your doctor, maybe a nutritionist, maybe a personal trainer, and certainly scads and scads of fans like your family and friends (online or in person) who can push you, support you, and yank the bowl of candy corn away from you. But you shouldn't be the only one relying on other people; you should use this opportunity to find a support partner who needs you as much as you need her. After all, the best kinds of satisfaction shouldn't come from the sixth spoonful of cake batter, but from sharing knowledge and support, and helping others lose inches.

6. Small Changes = Long-Term Success

The average woman gains 24 pounds between the ages of twenty-five and sixty-five. Considering that the total food intake of a woman over forty is more than 40,000 pounds of food in the rest of her lifetime, the difference between food intake and food expenditure that produces such a weight gain is .06 percent — or just 8 calories a day. And if you want to lose weight, the whole fight comes down to a measly 100 calories a day — that's 10 permanent pounds and roughly 3 inches off your waist every year.

FOOD

7. You Need to Eat to Lose Weight

We know exactly how you've felt when you've dieted in the past. Hungry. Famished. Three seconds away from steamrolling through a triple-dip cone with sprinkles. That recipe for dieting is one you can tear up. In fact, the only place hunger ever got you was a pair of pants that could double as curtains. To eat and work smart, your goal is *never* to be hungry and *never* to be in a state of dietary angst, where your only salvation is the 99-cent

20

menu at the drive-through window. By keeping your hunger (and internal chemicals) in check by feeding — not starving — your body, you'll avoid the impetuous behaviors that send fat on an express ride to your belly.

8. Make Good Choices Automatic, Not a Chore

If your waist management plan is going to work — as in, really work, for your whole life — then eating right has to become as automatic as it was for our ancestors. That's not as insurmountable as it seems. Just look at one study from the *Journal of the American Medical Association.* Two groups were assigned two different diets. One went on a diet rich with good-for-you foods like whole grains, fruits, vegetables, nuts, and olive oil, foods found in the typical Mediterranean diet. The other group was not given any specific direction in terms of foods to eat but was instructed to consume specific percentages of fat, carbohydrates, and protein daily. In short, they had to think a lot about preparing foods and dividing amounts, while the first group only had general guidelines about foods to eat. The groups weren't given directions about how much to eat; they let their hunger levels dictate their hunger patterns. And when they did that, what happened? Without trying, the first group ate fewer calories, lost inches, and dropped pounds.

9. Get to Know the Two Hunger Hormones

In sumo champions, a little extra fat

can produce good results. But we also think that fat has an unfair knock against it. Fat is treated a little like an accused suspect; it sometimes gets a bum rap. Fat produces a chemical signal in your blood that tells you to stop eating. Left to its own devices, fat is self-regulating; the problem occurs when we override our internal monitoring system and continue to stuff ourselves long after we're no longer hungry. Your body knows when it's had enough, and it prevents you from wanting any more food on top of that. How does fat curb appetite? Through one of the most important chemicals in the weight-reduction process: leptin, a protein secreted by stored fat. The challenge is to let leptin do its job so that the brain demands less food. One way to do it: Walk thirty minutes a day and build a little muscle. When you lose some weight, your cells become more sensitive and responsive to leptin. Your stomach and intestines do more than hold food and produce Richter-worthy belches. When your stomach's empty, they release a feisty little chemical called ghrelin. When your stomach's growling, it's this gremlin of a hormone that's controlling your body's offense; it sends desperate messages that you need more points, you need to score, you need to FedEx the chili dogs to the GI tract immediately.

Ghrelin makes you want to eat. To make things worse, when you diet through deprivation, the increased ghrelin secretion sends even more signals to eat, overriding your willpower and causing chemical reactions that give you little choice but to line your tongue with bits of beef jerky. Ghrelin also promotes eating by increasing the secretion of growth hormone. So when you increase ghrelin levels, you stimulate that growth hormone to kick in, and growth hormone builds you not only up but out as well. Your stomach secretes ghrelin in pulses every half hour, sending subtle chemical impulses to your brain — almost like subliminal biological messages (carrot cake, carrot cake, carrot cake). When you're really hungry or dieting, those messages come fast — every twenty minutes or so — and they're also amplified. So you get more signals and stronger signals that your body wants food. After long periods, your body can't ignore those messages. That's why sugar cookies usually trump willpower, and that's why deprivation dieting can never work: It's impossible to fight the biology of your body. The chemical vicious cycle stops when you eat; when your stomach fills is when you reduce your ghrelin levels, thus reducing your appetite. So if you think your job is to resist biology, you're going to lose that battle time after time. But if you can reprogram your body so that you keep those ghrelin gremlins from making too much noise, then you've got a chance to keep your tank feeling like it's always topped off.

A major gang leader against your body is fructose, found in high-fructose corn syrup (HFCS), a sweetener in many processed foods. If you can avoid fructose and eat the healthy foods we outline below, you'll let leptin do its job and keep ghrelin from doing its damage.

10. Learn Your Nutrients

Contrary to popular belief, not all ingested protein becomes muscle, and not all the fat in your food gets stored on your hips. Everything has the potential to turn into fat if it's not used by your body for energy at the exact time it is absorbed through your intestines. And energy is energy is energy. Here's how the different nutrients are processed:

Simple sugars (as in a cola): When sugar, which is quickly absorbed and sent to the liver, meets the liver in the digestion process, the liver tells your body to turn that sugar into a fat if it can't be used immediately for energy.

Complex carbohydrates (as in whole grain foods): They take longer to digest, so there's a slower release of the carbohydrates that have been converted in your bowel to sugar to become sugar in your bloodstream. That means your digestive system is not stressed as much. Still, if your body can't use this slower sugar when it's released, it gets converted to fat.

Protein (as in meat): It gets broken down into small amino acids, which then go to the liver. If the liver can't send them to your muscles (say, if you're not exercising and don't need them for muscle growth or maintenance), then, yep, they get converted to glucose, which then gets converted to fat if you can't use it for energy.

Fat (as in funnel cake): It gets broken into smaller particles of fat and gets absorbed as fat. Good fats (like those found in nuts and fish) decrease your body's inflammatory response, and bad fats increase it. That inflammatory response is a contributing factor to obesity and its complications. If you're exercising and have used up all readily available carbohydrates (sugar), your muscles can use fat for energy, which is a great way to erode your love handles.

11. Read Labels Regularly

You should read food labels as actively as you read the stock ticker or the horoscopes. We have a *YOU: On a Diet* "Rule of 5s." If any food has any one of the five ingredients below as any one of the first five ingredients on the label, don't let it near your mouth.

- ❑ Simple sugars
- ❑ Enriched, bleached, or refined flour (this means it's stripped of its nutrients)
- ❑ All syrups, including HFCS (high-fructose corn syrup — a four-letter word)
- ❑ Saturated fat (four-legged animal fat or palm or coconut oil)
- ❑ Trans fat (partially hydrogenated vegetable oil)

Putting them into your body is like dunking your cell phone in a glass of water. It'll cause your system to short out your hormones and send your body confusing messages about eating. When typical slightly overweight people eat sugar, they on average store 5 percent as ready energy to use later, metabolize 60 percent, and store a whopping 35 percent as fat that can be converted to energy later. Any guess as to where 50 percent of the sugar we consume comes from? HFCS in fat-free foods like salad dressings and regular soft drinks.

12. Don't Confuse Thirst with Hunger

The reason some people eat is because the satiety centers in their brains are begging for attention. But sometimes those appetite centers want things to quench thirst, not to fill the stomach. Thirst could be caused by hormones in the gut, or it could be a chemical response to eating; eating food increases the thickness of your blood, and your body senses the need to dilute it. A great way to counteract your hormonal reaction to food is to make sure that your response to thirst activation doesn't contain unnecessary, empty calories — like the ones in soft drinks or alcohol. Your thirst center doesn't care whether it's getting zero-calorie water or a megacalorie frappé. When you feel hungry, drink a glass or two of water first, to see if that's really what your body wants.

Good Foods/Nutrients!

❑ Lean proteins (chicken and turkey, fish like salmon)
❑ Healthy fats (olive oil, nuts)
❑ 100 percent whole grains
❑ Fruits and vegetables
❑ Foods with fiber

13. Slow Down the Eating Process

If you have a little of the right kinds of fat just before you eat, you can trick your hormonal system by sending the signal to your brain that you're full. If you eat a little fat twenty-five minutes before your meal (70 calories or so of fat in the form of six walnut halves, twelve almonds, or twenty peanuts), you'll stimulate a chemical that will both communicate with your brain and slow your stomach from emptying to keep you feeling full. (It takes about twenty-five minutes to kick in and takes about 65 calories of fat to stimulate.) That way, you'll be able to sit down for a meal and eat for pleasure, not for hunger — which is one way to ensure you'll eat less. The average person is finished eating well before his satiety signals kick in, thus counteracting any possibility that his hormones can help him. For the same reason, you should eat slowly. If you down your food faster than a Mini-Vac, you won't allow your satiety hormones time to kick in.

14. Don't Hold Grudges Against Nuts

Eating nuts does not create the calorie intake that you might expect, because 5 to 15 percent of the calories are not absorbed by the intestinal system. That's because the nuts' skin and how well we chew nuts influence digestion. An added bonus: The slow release of calories throughout the intestinal system leads to prolonged satiety.

15. Small Plates Will Change Your Life

Monstrous portion sizes are one of our stomach's biggest enemies: Studies show that when you're served bad foods in large containers, you'll eat up to one-third more than if you were served in smaller containers. By getting served in larger popcorn boxes, bigger dishes, and taller cups, we've automatically been tricked into thinking that availability should dictate how much we eat, rather than physical hunger. You don't have to go through drastic changes to make small ones. For starters, change your serving plates to the 9-inch variety to give yourself the visual and psychological cue that you're full when your physical appetite has been sated. That's important, because studies show visual cues help determine how full you are, in that you may not feel satisfied until your plate is clean, no matter how large the plate is. That's also reason never to eat directly out of a box or carton and always to remember that one serving size of a food is often about the size of a fist.

16. Go Through the Process of Elimination

To change the way you feel, the way you process food, and the way you store fat is to get at the root of the system: You need to figure out what foods may be causing you gastrointestinal (GI) trouble, no matter how subtle your symptoms may be. The best way to do that is through the food-elimination test. What you'll do is completely eliminate certain groups of foods for at least three days in a row. (Sometimes, the elimination of a food takes two or more weeks to show its benefits in how you feel.) During that time, take notes about all the different ways you feel: your energy levels, fatigue, and how often you go to the bathroom. Take notes when you eliminate foods and when you reintroduce them — that way you'll really notice what changes make you feel worse or better. Here's the order we suggest: wheat products (including rye, barley, and oats; see our G-Free Plan in *YOU: On a Diet,* revised edition), dairy products; refined carbohydrates (especially sugar); saturated and trans fats; and artificial colors (which are tough to get rid of because they're in everything). While the experiment will help you ID your personal digestive destructors, it has an added benefit: Eliminating a group of foods for several days at a time will help train your body to eat smaller portions all the time.

17. Add Some Pepper

Red pepper, when eaten early in the day, decreases food intake later in the day. Some credit the ingredient capsaicin for being the catalyst for decreasing overall calorie intake and for increasing metabolism. It also appears to work by inhibiting sensory information from the intestines from reaching the brain, which is particularly effective in reducing appetite in low-fat diets. Capsaicin works by killing — or at least stunning — the messages that you're hungry. So add red pepper to your egg-white omelet.

18. Drink Up

To help curb hunger and avoid binge eating, drink a glass or two of water before you eat.

19. Change the Temptation When Eating Out

Eating out at a colorful fast-food joint is like rowing out to a hurricane. The savory foods will flip you like a tidal wave. So the first trick to eating out is choosing a place that offers many healthy options (or will make them for you). You should be especially aware of danger zones — such as the first ten minutes of the meal (order veggies and olive oil, instead of bread) and the last ten minutes (have your glass of wine at the end of the meal, rather than a slab of chocolate mousse cake). Most will help. If there is a chef, just ask. Can you make that veggie burger without sauce? Can you make that veggie sub without cheese, oil, or mayo? Can you give me extra veggies instead of those potatoes? Can you give me cut-up veggies instead of a bread basket?

20. Keep Emergency Foods On Hand

Bad foods aren't bad just because of the ingredients they contain but also because many of them are fast and easy, which are the exact traits that can get you into a whole lot of trouble. The key to successful dietary contingency plans is to have premade foods ready for those times when you've been conditioned to reach for bags of sugar-containing waist build-ers. Instead, choose your favorites of these options to make once a week so you'll have something to grab when you need it.

Cut-up vegetables: Your choice. Cut them, bag them, eat them. Nothing wrong with baby carrots, grape tomatoes, and broccoli florets, but if you prefer jicama, sugar snaps, and orange pepper strips, go for it.

Sautéed vegetables: Your choice. Sauté them in olive oil with chopped garlic, red pepper flakes, or a good dash of turmeric. Refrigerate and use for side dishes or hot (microwaved) snacks.

Soups: Make one or more of our filling healthy soups once a week and store them in serving-size cups in the refrigerator. Eat 1 cup as a predinner appetizer, to take the edge off, or have a cup of soup as a snack.

Steel-cut oats: If you're worried about time, cook up one week's worth of oats per directions and store in the refrigerator for up to a week. For some people, that may seem as appetizing as a slice of baked wrapping paper, but reheated oats actually taste great.

Emergency foods: Every house needs fire-extinguisher foods — good-for-you foods that will put out three-alarm starvation fires. Our list of foods that you can reach for when you're hungry include any of the above foods as well as a handful of almonds, peanuts, or walnuts; bags of store-bought, prechopped fruits and veggies; dried fruit (apricots, cranberries); and edamame (soybeans — look for microwave bags in the frozen food section). Avoid the foods with added sugars. In a real pinch? Pop one of those mint breath strips — they can help turn off appetite by making food less appetizing.

21. Learn to Decipher Jargon, Part I

Nowadays, foods have more labels than a clothes rack, ingredient names look like the names of Greek goddesses, and cunning marketing lingo makes sugar-drenched cereal appear as if it's healthier than a bundle of prunes. And that's just not the case. Prince Nutrition sounds great until you read the label and find no nutrient other than sugar and saturated fat, which have been neatly disguised under unrecognizable names. The trick to navigating through store aisles is not only to shop for value and whisk the kids past the Admiral Nutrition candy bars and potato chips but also to shop for content — for the ingredients and nutrients that allow you to eat smart, not diet hard. Here is our guide for ingredient inspection:

Look for less: Generally, fewer labels and ingredients equal better foods. Natural foods that come directly from the ground generally don't require labels. (Ever seen a marshmallow bush?) That's why any produce is generally OK for you. (One caveat: Make sure it has a great feel, a healthy smell, and has not been waxed; waxed versions are like a Barbie doll — look great, but not much substance. These versions often have less taste and less nutrition.)

Turn the package: Ignore what's on the front of the package and go directly to the food label and ingredient list. "Fat-free!" or "zero trans fats" may sound like a dieter's dream, but fat-free foods (especially salad dressing) can be loaded with more sugar than a baker's bowl. Another caution: Just because something "contains whole grains" doesn't mean it's made entirely or even mostly with whole grains. Bottom line: The front of the package isn't even as revealing as the outside of a new car. It might look seductive, but you really have to check what's under the hood to see what it's all about. The ingredient list is where all the answers are.

Beware of the imposters: Many foods contain cheat words in their ingredient list — the words don't clearly scream "imminent heart attack!" as some other words may, but they indicate danger all the same. Some notable clues to watch for:

❑ *For sugar:* Dextrose, sucrose, or anything with "ose." And mannitol, or anything with "ol." Those are alcohols that are quickly converted to sugar. Stay away from foods that have more than 4 grams of sugar per serving in them. Even natural sugars such as maple syrup and molasses are sugar, so you should also keep them to fewer than 4 grams per serving, unless it's pure fruit (we make that exception because fruit has so many nutrients).

❑ *For fats:* Besides saturated fats (fewer than 4 grams per serving) and trans fats (avoid them all), you should avoid foods with other fat code words, like partially hydrogenated, palm, and coconut oil.

Relax. We don't want you to spend more time in the store than you did in freshman economics class. If you haven't inspected labels before, it'll just take some time before you know exactly how to ID the nutritional heroes and the imposters. We also don't want you to be a paranoid

shopper or paranoid about eating
— some dangerous-sounding foods
such as walnuts or real peanut butter
or even honey (fewer than 4 grams
per serving here) are OK in modera-
tion.

22. Learn to Decipher Jargon, Part II

It used to be that the only thing
with a hole in it was a doughnut.
Now, it seems, everything is touted as
"whole" this or that. Whole grains,
whole wheat, a whole lot of health:
It's the latest in food marketing. Why?
Because food manufacturers know
that whole grains are, in fact, one
of the healthiest ingredients you can
eat. Getting your whole grain fibers
to be greater than 25 grams a day
(from either 100 percent whole grains

such as wheat or oats or barley or psyllium) reduces your overall risk of death by over 60 percent in the next ten years. Sure, more and more foods are made with them, but that doesn't mean all are created equal. Why? Because those marketing words don't always present an accurate picture of what's inside the food. To decipher the whole mess, you first need to understand what exactly whole grains are and how they work. "Whole grain" means the grain still has all three of its original elements: the outer shell or bran, which contains fiber and B vitamins, the germ, which contains phytochemicals and B vitamins; and the endosperm (what a name), which contains carbohydrates and protein. The key is that they're "whole" and not "refined," by stripping away the bran and germ, which leaves you eating only the aptly named endosperm. Instead, the whole grain should be left intact — meaning you get more fiber and more micronutrients that help protect against disease. These whole grains are also healthy for you because they're absorbed more slowly than enriched or bleached flour and thus raise glucose and insulin levels less — keeping you fuller longer and slowing your digestion. But not all foods that tout whole grains or whole wheat are the healthiest form. Some fake-out words you should watch out for:

Made with: It may have a drop of whole grains, but unless it's made entirely with them, you won't reap all the potential benefits.

100 percent wheat: This means it could have some or a lot or no "whole" wheat.

Multigrain: This tells you nothing about whether the grains are whole or refined. Even if you're getting thirty-eight grains, that isn't much good if they are all refined.

Whole grain: If the label doesn't say "100 percent whole grain," it may have many blends. Bad words to see: *enriched, bleached, unbleached, semolina, durum,* and *rice flour.*

Blends: "Whole grain blend" means it usually doesn't have much whole grain at all.

Good source: This means it has 8 grams of whole grains per serving or as little as 13.5 percent. Don't confuse whole grain with fiber; 8 grams of whole grain may have less than 1 gram of fiber.

Excellent source: This means it has 16 grams per serving or as little as 27 percent.

Supports heart health: Any food can say that it "supports" an organ. What you want to see on the label: "May reduce the risk of . . ." This means that the food has ingredients clinically shown to be effective in reducing the risk of, say, heart disease or high cholesterol, depending on the food (like whole — not instant — oats and psyllium husks do).

23. Minimize Damage at Fast-Food Places

We understand how it is. Sometimes you need the absolute quickest path from food to belly. While most fast-food options are more destructive than a 4 a.m. vandal, you can still make smart choices in the drive-through lane. Some things to remember:

❏ There are some main dishes that can be good for you, but you have to be careful. Some slight name variations can make the difference between causing your fat and keeping you flat.

❏ Avoid side dishes and desserts unless indicated below. They're all loaded with bad fats and simple sugars, and they often have more calories than the main dishes.

- ❑ Choose low-calorie dressing, not low-fat. Low-fat dressings are steeped in HFCS, which has plenty of calories, and the fructose tricks your body into staying hungry.
- ❑ Don't eat breakfast at fast-food places. There are virtually no healthy options on any breakfast menu we could find.

24. Navigate the Dangerous Territory of Eating Out

Eating out can be a great experience — for everyone except your gut. With Rushmore-sized portions and dietary disasters in every plate, basket, and spoonful, restaurants are dangerous places. While you should always follow our guidelines for good foods (the waist foods, not the waste foods, in our crib sheet), you should also know that most dietary mistakes are made within the first and last ten minutes of any restaurant experience. Some tips for bookending your meal the right way:

❑ Return the free bread and ask if you can have cut-up raw vegetables instead. (Do this four times in a three-week period, and we've found that most good restaurants remember the trick and automatically make that change every time they see you — if they see you at least once a week.)

❑ Order oil and vinegar in separate containers and on the side for salad dressing, and put a little on. (You have to do this; relying on the waitstaff or chef to do so gets you about 400 extra calories per side salad.)

❑ Ask to replace the potato or rice with sautéed vegetables.

❑ If you're going to have dessert, order one for the table and have just a few bites.

25. Avoid This Four-Letter Word: HFCS

High-fructose corn syrup (HFCS) — once considered the "Frankenfood" fueling America's obesity epidemic — recently earned a presidential-style pardon. The American Medical Association concluded last June that this much-maligned sweetener was no worse than sugar. Recently, in *The*

American Journal of Clinical Nutrition, a group of noted nutrition experts who've studied this processed sweet stuff agreed. Even if you don't read medical journals or follow the headlines, you've probably seen the pro-HFCS commercials on TV — paid for by the Corn Refiners Association — featuring smiling moms reassuring one another that HFCS is perfectly safe and natural. (Of course, cyanide is also natural. Not that taking HFCS is the equivalent of ingesting cyanide, but don't think it has a clean bill of health.)

Hold that honey-mustard dipping sauce. Who said sugar was a great item to add to food? Further, almost all of the reports that found HFCS to be the same as sugar have been funded by groups that profit from sales of

HFCS — including soda makers and their lobbyists. And we believe that the most important question remains whether big doses of fructose could trigger obesity in ways that go beyond all those excess calories.

Yes, we said fructose. But we don't mean the quantities found in fresh fruit, which come packaged with fiber and lots of nutrients. We're talking about the nutritionally empty megadoses added to soda, commercial sweets, and baked goods. We're also talking about all the little hits you're getting from foods that don't even seem sweet, such as ketchup and salad dressing. A growing stack of research suggests that getting too much fructose in your diet interferes with telling your brain that you're full and should stop eating. In a new University of

Florida lab study, animals that ate a high-fat, high-calorie diet that was also high in fructose became leptin resistant (resistant to changes leptin causes in the brain, such as ability to suppress appetite) and gained more weight than animals that ate a similar diet, minus the fructose. And fructose in large quantities overwhelms your liver's ability to process it without producing inflammation-producing compounds.

Truth is, HFCS isn't the only source of excess fructose in the American diet. Table sugar has a similar makeup (roughly equal amounts of fructose and glucose). The reason HFCS comes under such fire is that the food industry's been pumping more and more of it into foods since the 1970s because it's cheap, mixes easily into beverages, and enhances flavor and shelf life. The result: we eat 1,000 times more HFCS now than when Richard Nixon was president — on average 63 pounds a year! That's over 230,000 calories worth. Per person! Per year! The greatest cost differential in our global fight for jobs is health care costs: Health care costs are twice as expensive in America as in Europe since we have twice the chronic disease. Food choices, physical inactivity, tobacco, and stress cause 70 percent of those chronic diseases. So if all you care about is the potential for jobs in America, you'd ban tobacco and simple sugars like HFCS added to your foods.

The bottom line: Getting the obvious, and not so obvious, sweeteners out of your diet will save you hundreds of calories a day — and remove a substance that could be flipping metabolic switches without your permission.

Here's how:

❑ Say no to soda and other sweetened drinks. The calories alone are enough reason to stop sipping liquid candy: A single 18-ounce soda, sweet iced tea, or fruit drink can pack 200 or more calories — courtesy of the 15 teaspoons of sugarlike sweetener, usually HFCS, these beverages contain.

❑ If you're breaking a serious soda habit, transitioning to an artificially sweetened, 0-calorie version is a good stepping-stone on your way to healthier drinks: unsweetened iced tea, tea, black coffee, or skim milk. (Yes, coffee and tea are much healthier, according to much scientific data not sponsored by those who might profit from such.)

❏ Read labels to find hidden HFCS. Check the ingredients lists of all the processed foods you buy for HFCS (as well as other sweeteners you don't need, such as rice syrup). You'll find HFCS in many breads, sweetened yogurts, and condiments. Buy only the brands without 'em, and certainly without them in the first five ingredients.

26. to 35. Enjoy These Recipes

Below, you'll find some of our favorite easy, healthy, tasty recipes. You can find dozens more in the full version of *YOU: On a Diet* (and the full nutritionals: these all meet our healthy for you — and your waist — guidelines).

Magical Breakfast Blaster
2 servings ❖ 136 calories per serving

1/2 large ripe banana, broken into chunks (or other fruit of your choice)

1 scoop (1/3 cup) Soy Protein (like Nature's Plus Spiru-Tein: naturesplus.com)

1/2 tablespoon flaxseed oil

1/4 cup frozen blueberries

1/2 tablespoon apple juice concentrate or honey

1 teaspoon psyllium seed husks
8 ounces water

Combine all ingredients in a blender. Optional: Add a few cubes of ice, as well as powdered vitamins. Cover; blend until fairly smooth.

Lifestyle 180 Chia Muffins
Makes 12–14 muffins ❖ 150 calories per muffin

1 tablespoon ground chia seeds
1 1/2 cups whole wheat flour
2 teaspoons ground cinnamon
1/2 teaspoon ground nutmeg
2 teaspoons baking soda
1/2 teaspoon salt
15 ounces canned pumpkin
1/4 cup canola oil
2 tablespoons agave nectar

1 tablespoon vanilla extract

3/4 cup chopped walnuts

1/4 cup water or no-sugar-added
  apple juice

1 cup fresh apple, peeled and grated
  on the large-hole side of the grater
  (5 1/2 ounces by weight)

Preheat oven to 350°F. Combine the chia seeds, flour, cinnamon, nutmeg, baking soda, and salt and mix with a wire whisk. In a separate bowl combine pumpkin, canola oil, agave nectar, vanilla, walnuts, and water or juice, mix, and then fold into dry ingredients. Fold in the grated apple. Scoop into paper cups in muffin tins and bake for 33 minutes, or until inserted toothpick comes out clean. Remove from muffin tin and cool on wire rack.

Lifestyle 180 Vita-Mix Green Smoothie

3 servings ❖ 120 calories per serving

2 cups ice

1/2 cup cold water

1/2 cup packed spinach leaves

1 cup chopped cooked kale leaves

1 orange, peeled and seeded

1 cup green seedless grapes

1 small ripe pear, peeled and cut into chunks

1 large banana, peeled and broken into chunks

2 teaspoons chia seeds

Combine all ingredients in a blender. Cover and blend until fairly smooth.

NOTE: We often add a teaspoon of psyllium husks to this to increase our

100 percent whole grain fiber and decrease LDL cholesterol.

Garden Harvest Soup
10 servings (about 1 cup each) ❖ 176 calories per serving

1 tablespoon extra-virgin olive oil

1 medium onion, chopped

1 carrot, chopped

4 garlic cloves, thinly sliced

1 red bell pepper, chopped

2 quarts (8 cups) low-salt vegetable or chicken stock or broth

1 can (28 ounces) whole, crushed, or diced tomatoes, undrained

2 cups water

1 small head cabbage, thinly sliced

1/2 teaspoon hot red pepper sauce (optional)

Salt and freshly ground black pepper

(optional)
Optional garnishes: chopped fresh parsley, chopped fresh cilantro

Heat a large saucepan over medium-high heat. Add oil, then onion; cook 5 minutes, stirring occasionally. Stir in carrot, garlic, and bell pepper; cook until tender. Add stock, tomatoes, water, and cabbage; simmer uncovered 20 minutes. Season to taste with hot sauce and salt and pepper if desired. Garnish with parsley or cilantro if desired.

Lisa's Great Gazpacho
4 servings (about 1 cup each) ❖ 120 calories per serving

1 can (28 ounces) crushed or diced tomatoes, undrained

1 cup tomato juice

1 cup each: diced (1/4 inch) red
   or orange bell pepper, unpeeled
   cucumber

1/4 cup finely chopped red onion

2 green onions, finely chopped

1 bunch cilantro leaves, chopped

3 tablespoons red wine vinegar or
   apple cider vinegar

3 tablespoons extra-virgin olive oil

2 dashes (or to taste) hot red pepper
   sauce

2 garlic cloves, minced

Salt and freshly ground black pepper
   (optional)

Optional garnishes: chopped fresh
   parsley, diced avocado

Place all ingredients except salt, pepper, and garnishes in large bowl and
combine. Coarsely puree about half

the mixture in a blender or food processor and return it to the bowl; stir well. Season to taste with salt and pepper if desired. Refrigerate for at least 2 hours and up to 8 hours before serving. Garnish as desired.

Asian Salmon with Brown Rice Pilaf

4 servings ❖ 674 calories per serving

Brown Rice
1 tablespoon extra-virgin olive oil
1/2 onion, chopped
1/2 red bell pepper, chopped
2 cups water
1 cup uncooked short-grain brown rice
1/4 cup finely chopped parsley
Salt and freshly ground black pepper (optional)

Salmon Ingredients

4 skinless salmon fillets (about 4
  ounces each)
1 tablespoon extra-virgin olive oil
1 garlic clove, pressed or minced
1 tablespoon grated fresh ginger
1 teaspoon soy sauce
1 teaspoon maple syrup
2 green onions, chopped

To make the rice, heat oil in a medium saucepan. Add onion and bell pepper; cook 3 minutes. Add water and rice; bring to a boil. Reduce heat; cover and simmer 50 minutes, or until rice is tender and liquid is absorbed. Fluff with a fork; stir in parsley. Season with salt and pepper if desired. Meanwhile, place salmon in a pie plate or shallow dish. Combine remaining salmon ingredients; mix well. Pour marinade over salmon; let stand 15 to 20 minutes. Heat a ridged grill pan over medium heat until hot. Add salmon, discarding marinade; cook 3 to 4 minutes per side, or until salmon is opaque and firm to the touch. Serve with brown rice.

Spicy Chili
4 servings ❖ 390 calories per serving

1 tablespoon extra-virgin olive oil
1/2 pound ground turkey or ground meat substitute (such as Boca Ground Crumbles)
1/2 onion, chopped
2 garlic cloves, minced
1 can (28 ounces) crushed tomatoes, undrained
1 can (16 ounces) kidney beans, drained
1/2 teaspoon chili powder

Pinch of cayenne pepper
1 teaspoon maple syrup
1 teaspoon wine vinegar
1/2 teaspoon ground coriander
1/2 teaspoon turmeric
Brown Rice Pilaf (recipe on page 70)

Heat oil in a large saucepan. Add turkey, onion, and garlic; cook 5 minutes, stirring frequently. Add remaining ingredients; simmer uncovered 25 minutes.

Stuffed Whole Wheat Pizza
4 servings ❖ (2 slices per serving); for the first two weeks, you can have up to half of the pizza, but most will not need that much to be full • 322 calories per serving

Cooking oil spray
1 pound fresh stir-fry vegetables

such as asparagus, broccoli,
cauliflower, mushrooms,
multicolored bell peppers, red and
white onions, and zucchini, cut up
2 garlic cloves, minced
Salt and freshly ground black pepper
(optional)
1 cup pizza sauce or tomato sauce
2 tablespoons olive relish or
tapenade
2 tablespoons sundried-tomato bits
One 12-inch or 10-ounce prepared
thin 100 percent whole wheat pizza
crust
1/2 cup (2 ounces) finely shredded
part-skim mozzarella cheese

Heat oven to 425°F. Heat a large nonstick skillet over medium-high heat until
hot; coat with cooking spray. Add vegetables and garlic; stir-fry (really sauté)

2 to 5 minutes, or until vegetables are crisp-tender.

Season to taste with salt and pepper if desired. Combine pizza sauce, olive relish, and sundried-tomato bits. Spread over pizza crust; top with cooked vegetables and cheese. Bake pizza directly on oven rack 10 to 15 minutes, or until crust is golden brown and cheese is melted. Cut pizza into 8 wedges.

Sliced Peaches with Raspberries, Blueberries, and Chocolate Chips

2 servings ❖ 46 calories per serving

2 small ripe peaches, sliced
1/2 teaspoon ground cinnamon
Pinch of nutmeg
1/4 cup (1 ounce) fresh raspberries
1/4 cup (1 ounce) fresh blueberries

1 1/2 tablespoons mini semisweet chocolate chips

Combine sliced peaches with cinnamon and nutmeg; transfer to two serving plates. Top peaches with raspberries, blueberries, and chocolate chips.

Lifestyle 180 Chia Banana Cake
24 squares 130 calories per square

1 tablespoon chia seeds
1/2 cup water
4 very ripe bananas
1 teaspoon vanilla extract
1/4 cup canola oil
5 tablespoons agave nectar
1 1/4 cups water
2 cups whole wheat flour
2 teaspoons baking powder

1 teaspoon baking soda
1 teaspoon salt
1 teaspoon cinnamon
1/2 cup chopped toasted walnuts

Combine in small mixing bowl the chia seeds and 1/4 cup water, mix well, and set at room temperature for 15 minutes to allow chia seeds to swell. While chia seeds are swelling, in another large bowl combine peeled banana, vanilla, canola oil, and agave nectar and mix with electric mixer until the mixture is very smooth with no lumps. Once chia seeds have swelled, add to banana mixture and blend well. Add remaining 1 cup water and mix with electric mixer until well blended. In a large bowl, combine whole wheat flour, baking powder, baking soda, salt, and cinnamon and mix with a wire whisk. Slowly add dry ingredients to wet ingredients in one-third increments while mixing with electric mixer until well blended before adding more. After all of the dry ingredients are added and well blended, add walnuts, mix well, and pour into a 9x13-inch lined and sprayed nonstick baking pan. Bake in a 350°F oven for 30 minutes or until a toothpick comes out clean. Allow to cool, cut into squares, and serve.

ACTIVITY & EXERCISE

36. Know the Why Before the How

Exercise increases your metabolism so that you burn energy at a higher rate than if you didn't exercise, and it reduces your appetite by turning on your sympathetic nervous system, which activates your fight-or-flight response. Do the experiment yourself. Take a quick walk or jog when you feel the first twinge of hunger. Presto, your hunger is gone when you return.

❑ Exercise will help you lose the extra weight that's stressing your joints. By dropping weight, you'll feel less pain in your knees, hips, ankles, and back. And that will put you into a positive cycle of behavior, so that you'll have the desire to exercise more.

❑ Exercise stimulates the release of endorphins, which stimulate the pleasure centers in the brain. When they're stimulated, they give you a sense of control, which is associated with a decreased need to eat out of control.

❑ Exercise helps decrease depression and increases positive attitude, so you make other positive choices and don't have to use food as your medication. That will also help prevent your couch, chair, and bed from becoming anti-waist-management devices.

❑ Exercise keeps your blood vessels open and clog-free, thus decreasing your risk of obesity-related morbidities like high blood pressure, elevated lousy cholesterol, memory problems, and heart attacks.

37. Do Not Fear Almighty Muscle

Muscle serves as a primary energy consumer for your body. Think of it as a raging fire. Toss a log into it, and it'll burn the log up pretty quickly. But your fat is more like one lit match — it would take years for that match to burn the log. In your body, muscle can fry up that cheese dog a lot faster than can fat — thus reducing the amount of fat you store. Add just a little more muscle, and you'll use more energy and store less fat. And that makes it an even more efficient exercise for burning fat than cardio-vascular training. That's pretty crucial when you consider that we lose an average of 5 percent of our muscle mass every ten years after the age of thirty-five — if we don't do anything about it. (Historically, hunters, gatherers, and carriers of children needed their muscular strength until they were about thirty-five, when kids were able to walk and younger tribesmen could hunt. But after they turned thirty-five, their bodies didn't give two tubers about whether they had any muscle, so their bodies adapted and allowed for that gradual loss.) Today we see drastic effects when we lose muscle — we gain weight. If you don't intentionally rebuild muscle through exercise, every ten years you'll need to eat 120 to 420 fewer calories each day to maintain your current weight.

38. Think of the Whole, Not the Parts

Doing exercises for a particular body part will not burn fat at that very point. Your body decides where it wants to burn fat, so there's no such thing as spot-reduction through exercise. Otherwise, wouldn't we be seeing people doing double-chin crunches in the gym? Instead, by doing exercises for a specific body part, you're building muscle mass in that area — which, after burning fat, will have the appearance and attributes of lean, strong muscle.

39. Take the First Step

Here's what you need to do, activity-wise:

- ❏ thirty minutes of walking *a day* to help rebuild the stamina- and strength-based proteins. That prepares your muscles for . . .
- ❏ thirty minutes of strength/resistance training *a week* to rebuild the strength-based proteins. (That's once a week for thirty minutes, or split up into two fifteen-minute sessions or three ten-minute ones.)

40. And Add in a Little Stretching

Being flexible isn't just a good trait for yoga teachers and potential spouses; it's also what you want for your muscles. Good flexibility helps prevent injuries to your joints, because stretching works your muscles through a wide range of motion that you'll go through during exercise and everyday activity. Plus, being flexible just makes you feel better; it keeps your body from feeling stiffer than a week-old roach corpse, helps facilitate meditation, and allows you to center yourself as you focus on your body. Plus, the more pliable and loose you are, the less you're affected when you fall or get into accidents.

41. Don't Go Overboard, No Matter How Eager You Are

While exercise has more pluses than a math workbook, you can take it too far. Burning more than 6,500 calories a week through exercise (that's roughly thirteen hours) or doing more than two hours in a row of cardiovascular training can not only stress your joints (depending on the exercise), but it also appears to be the level at which you induce too much oxidative stress in your body, and that decreases your longevity.

42. Maintain Good Form

The steps to using good form while you do resistance-training moves.

1. Look out at eye level or above to spare your neck and keep you

from rolling your shoulders forward.

2. Assume the Botox pose: Keep your face relaxed and tension-free.

3. Relax your shoulders and lift up your chest.

4. Pretend the top of your head is being pulled up by a string to elongate your spine and keep you from rolling forward.

5. Count your reps of each exercise out loud; this counting will help you remember to breathe continuously and keep you from holding your breath.

6. Keep your abs tight and pulled in to support your lower back. (Practice sucking in every time you enter a car, bus, train, plane, elevator, escalator — that way it

becomes automatic.)

7. Keep your knees slightly bent, so you don't lock them.

8. When doing shoulder exercises, make sure you can always see your hands (if you wanted to).

9. Breathe. Many people hold their breath while doing strength training.

10. Keep moving in between exercises to keep your heart rate fast, or move directly to the next exercise.

    If you're unable to hold a conversation, you're exercising too hard. If you can keep a conversation going and are able to fill the listener in on all the details, you may not be going hard enough.

11. As you get stronger, go longer rather than harder with cardio ex-

ercises, and stronger with weight exercises. That is, do more repetitions of any non-weight-bearing exercise. That will help prevent injuries from overexertion. If you really feel weak, just hold the exercise position without moving and slowly work up. It's more important to follow perfect form and do fewer repetitions than to do a lot of repetitions with form that's sloppier than spaghetti in a high chair.

YES, we want you to add cardio — that is, exercise that makes you sweat in a cool room or raises your heart rate to 80+ percent of your age-adjusted max — 220 minus your age for men and 208 minus 82 percent of your age for women — with one minute of every ten going all out (if your doc says you can). The minimum cardio for maximum health benefit is 21 minutes three times a week, all done at 80+ percent of your age-adjusted max, including the last minute of every ten done as intensely as possible. But do cardio only after you have done at least 60 days of 10,000 steps a day and a month of resistance training. So first prepare yourself for resistance with walking.

43. Prepare to Perspire

Before beginning an exercise program, you need more than a Lycra top. Exercise isn't dangerous, but your risk of injury will be less if you live with a few principles to protect your muscles and your entire body.

Warm up: Before beginning any exercise, warm up your muscles for about five minutes to prevent injury. (Our workout below includes a warm-up.) Remember, your muscles are like spaghetti strands; they're pliable when they're warm, and more injury-prone if they're not. Jogging, brisk walking, cycling, or doing exercises with light weight or no weight will help prepare your muscles for activity. One good rule: Do the same exercise you will be doing but at a slower pace or with lighter weight. Your goal is to move your joints through the same range of motion as they will do with exercise — to raise your heart rate and to increase the temperature of your muscles, which will make them more viscous and less likely to be injured. Some advocate that at the end of exercise, you should cool down with a light jog, cycle, or walk, but there's no evidence that a cooldown will reduce injury or muscle soreness more than just stretching at the end. But if you are doing intense cardio exercise, you do need to do a cooldown, rather than stopping abruptly at the end of the workout. For a cooldown, do the same activity, like running, at a much slower pace than you were maintaining during your workout.

Focus on your muscles: Take special notice of where you tense up. You want to release tension in your body, not shift it somewhere else. Most commonly, people shift it to their shoulders and their foreheads. Notice this, breathe, and focus on the muscles you are working.

Listen to your body: Throughout stretching, make sure to keep breathing freely and slowly. If you ever feel pain during stretching, stop. (That's different from a little discomfort as you're loosening up; actual pain should be your warning to stop. We *want* burning in the muscles.)

Wear the right shoes: You'll need to invest in a good pair of lightweight running shoes for walking (the strength workout you should do barefoot, unless you use weights). Appropriate shoes are well cushioned and designed to handle the heel-to-toe movements for both walking and running. Best option: Go to a specialty running store, where the often underpaid salespeople are the experts; ask the pro there to analyze your stride and match up the best shoe for your feet.

44. Test Your Fitness Level

There are lots of ways to gauge progress on a weight-loss plan: inches lost, Wendy's coupons tossed. But you can also measure your fitness levels in different areas of activity. Use these tests to see how you stack up. (Before doing each test, make sure to properly warm up by walking or doing light exercise for at least five minutes.)

Cardiovascular: You can measure your heart's efficiency by measuring your heart rate *after* exercise. After exercising for a period of eighteen minutes at 80 to 85 percent of your age-adjusted max (that's 220 minus your age), do three minutes at your maximum heart rate, then stop and check your pulse. Your heart rate should decrease 66 beats or more after two minutes of stopping. Do not do this without approval of your doctor unless you do it regularly as part of your workout.

Muscular: To gauge upper-body muscular stamina, do the push-up test (men in standard form; women can do it with knees on the floor). A thirty-year-old man should be able to do at least thirty-five (five less every decade after that, until he reaches seventy). A thirty-year-old woman should be able to do forty-five with knees on the floor (five less every decade after until she reaches eighty).

Flexibility: Measure lower-back flexibility by sitting on the floor with your legs straight out in front of you and slightly spread apart. With one hand on top of the other and finger-tips lined up, lean forward and reach for your feet. Women forty-five and under should be able to reach two to four inches past their feet. Older women should be able to reach to the soles. Men aged forty-five and under should be able to reach to the soles. Older men should be able to come within three to four inches of the soles.

45. Reward Your Body in the Morning

If you want an energy boost and a great way to wake up (and strengthen) your body, try yoga's sun salutation.

1. Stand with feet touching. Bring

your hands together, palm to palm, fingertips pointing upward.

Make sure your weight is evenly distributed. Exhale. Raise your arms upward. Slowly bend backward, pulling your abs in and up, stretching arms above the head. Relax your neck. Inhale.

2. Exhale while you slowly bend forward until your hands are in line with your feet, touching your head to your knees if possible. Press your hands down, fingertips in line with toes (bend your knees if you have to), and touch the floor. Maintain a slight bend in the knees to take pressure off your back through your hamstrings, and extend and elongate your back, rather than arching it,

to avoid lower-back issues. Relax your neck and shoulders; let them dangle down toward the ground. Use their weight to stretch your spine.

3. Move into an up push-up position with your hands and toes on the floor and your back straight.

4. Lower your body to a down push-up position with your elbows bent and your body remaining in a straight position from your legs to your head.

5. As you inhale, raise your head and bend backward as far as possible while straightening your arms. To go deeper as you lift, arch backward and pull the top of your head up and out and come onto the top of your feet as you lift your pelvis off the

ground. The four points would be your two palms and two tops of your feet.

6. Keeping your arms straight, raise your hips into down dog, pressing your armpits toward your knees, and align your head with your arms. Exhale throughout movement.

7. Keeping your leg straight, raise your right leg so it stays in line with your spine. Raise the left leg your second time through the sequence.

8. Return transiently to down dog position. Lunge your right leg forward.

9. As you inhale, keep your hands and feet on the ground, with your right foot between your hands. Reverse legs the second

time through.

10. Raise your head and lift your hands straight up to the sky while maintaining the lunge position.

11. Open your hips by turning to the left and outstretching your arms right side forward and left side back so that they're parallel to the floor.

12. Bring feet together and stand up straight. Keeping your legs straight, bend at the waist and lower your upper body. Touch your head to your knees if possible. Exhale.

13. Return to position 1 by slowly rising, straightening your back into a standing pose. Stretch your arms above your head as you inhale. Exhale and then repeat the sequence so you can

work the opposite muscles.

46. Do the Two of the World's Greatest Exercises

Best of all, they don't require any equipment — just your own body.

Squats

Stand with your feet a little wider than shoulder width apart and with your hands holding weights or in *I Dream of Jeannie* style (elbows in line with shoulders, and hands crossed to opposite upper arm). Throughout, keep your elbows in line with your shoulders. Without curling your back, squat down to the point where your thighs are approximately parallel to the floor (or before that if you have knee or lower-back pain). It should feel like you're about to sit on the toilet seat, but just before your buns touch down. Pause, then rise up to the original starting position. Look forward throughout the movement. Keep your shoulders back and in line with your hips. Breathe in on the way down; breathe out on the way up. You can add resistance by holding dumb-bells or other objects. You can do squats over a chair or sofa for safety in case you fall back. For variety, hold the lowermost position and pulse for a count of thirty and then continue your reps.

Push-up Variations

You can do classic push-ups (with knees on ground if necessary), keeping your back straight. As you get stronger, you can try these add-ons:

❑ Get in down-dog position: hands and toes on the floor and butt high in the air, like an inverted V. Look two inches above your shoulder-width hands and bend your elbows only, dropping your forehead to where your eyes are looking. Then straighten your arms. Keep your body in down dog the entire time. Wear a weighted vest (available at most sports-equipment stores), which will increase the amount of resistance during the movement.

❑ Alternate lifting each foot a few inches off the floor and bending your knee on each repetition to incorporate balance into the exercise.

❑ One-arm push-ups. *Hooyah!*

47. to 63. Do the YOU Workout

This twenty-minute workout will strengthen and stretch your entire body — all without any equipment! Do the following movements in order. Make adjustments to time or repetitions as your ability level dictates. Each strength exercise is followed by a stretch to loosen the same muscle group and keep you limber. We recommend that women not do twisting during the menstrual period as the anterior cruciate ligaments (ACL) are vulnerable to injury at that time. See www.realage.com for video of each move.

1: Roll With It

Allows any kinks in your shoulders to be smoothed out.

Roll your shoulders forward for a

count of ten and back for ten. "Swim" shoulders back for ten and forward for ten. Your goal is to get full range of movement with your shoulders. Notice any areas that you don't move fluidly and try to open them up by relaxing as you move your hands in full circles. Between sets, get into the habit of rolling your shoulders five times forward and five times back.

2: The Chest Cross

Strengthens chest and shoulders

(A) Reach your arms as forward as possible at shoulder height, and twirl your hands back and forth like you have a tennis ball in your hands. (B) Then cross your straight arms in front of your chest in a series of quick horizontal motions with your palms facing each other (so they provide some wind resistance to your motion). (C) Next, move your hands rapidly up and down with your palms facing the floor. Try to do each of these variations twenty-five times.

3 (Stretch): The Clapper

Stretches chest

In a standing position and keeping your chest up, clap in front of you; then bring your hands behind your back and clap your hands together. Keep your hands as high as you can in front and back during the movement. Keep your chest lifted when clapping in back. Do ten times.

4 (Stretch): The Hippie

Stretches hips and hamstrings

With your feet flat on the ground, bend forward at your waist. Alternate bending one knee and keeping the other leg straight (but still keeping your feet flat), and let your head dangle down, releasing all your tension. Stretch each side for fifteen seconds.

5: Push-up Pride

Strengthens chest

Get in the appropriate "up" push-up position for you by either staying on your toes or keeping your knees on the ground. Lower yourself until your chest nearly touches the ground and push back up. As you straighten your elbows, push your spine toward the ceiling (to help engage your back muscles as well). Pull your heels away from your shoulders, keeping a long, solid body. Don't let your stomach hang down toward the ground; make your stomach active by pulling it in to support your lower back. This will help release any unnecessary tension on your lower back. Keeping your stomach tight in any exercise strengthens your belly muscles. If your lower back starts to hurt, raise your butt slightly and curl your tailbone by tightening your butt. Keep your chin slightly up and look six inches past your fingertips. This forces you to use your chest and not overextend your neck while doing push-ups. Do as many push-ups as you can (this is called exercising to failure, and it's what helps build strength proteins in your muscle). If these are too hard, just hold your chest off the ground without moving. Or you can do a pyramid push-up routine: Do five push-ups, then hold in the up position for five seconds. Then do four and hold for four in the up position, all the way down to one.

6 (Stretch): Pecs Flex

Stretches chest and arms

Sit up straight on your heels and interweave your fingers behind your butt, while keeping your arms straight. Lift your fingers up, knuckle side facing back, while opening your chest wide. Squeeze your shoulder blades together to open your chest more. Use your breath to your advantage here, by breathing into the muscles being stretched. Another option is to interweave your fingers behind your head and pull your hands away from your head. Face forward for all versions.

7: Steady on the Plank

Strengthens abs and shoulders

Get into a push-up position with your elbows and toes on the floor, while pushing the area between your shoulders toward the ceiling and keeping your stomach pulled in toward your lower back, to support it. Keep your buttocks tight and your eyes looking at the floor (ignore the fact that you suddenly realize you have to vacuum). Hold the position for as long as you can. If you can last more than one minute, make it more difficult by dropping your chin twenty times out in front of interwoven hands, or by trying to balance on one foot.

8: Whose Side Are You On, Anyway?

Strengthens obliques (the muscles at the side of your abdominals)

Turn to the side by putting an

elbow on the floor and rotating the opposite hip toward the ceiling in a lateral plank. Keep your body in a straight line and resist pushing your butt back. Keep your abs tight as you hold the position for as long as you can. Alternate sides. If you can hold for more than one minute, you can increase the difficulty by repeatedly dropping your hip, tapping it on the mat, and bringing it back into the lateral plank.

9 (Stretch): Up, Dog, Up

Stretches abdominals and obliques

From a down push-up position, with your hands below your shoulders, lift your chest and torso up into the air so that your upper body is nearly perpendicular to the floor as you come onto the tops of your bare feet. Lean backward to stretch your abdominals, but keep your butt relaxed. Hold for ten seconds. Then look over your right shoulder for ten, then your left shoulder for ten, then back to center.

10: The Rickety Table

Strengthens upper back and butt

Put your hands and knees flat on the floor with your fingers spread apart and pointing directly forward. Keep your back flat and parallel to the floor and your supporting elbow slightly bent. Look down six inches above your fingertips. Reach your right hand forward and your left foot back and stretch them as far away from each other as possible, keeping your right hand higher than your head. The higher your arm goes up, the more work your back has to do, and the more effective the exercise. Now bring your right elbow to your left knee. Do twenty on this side, then alternate and do it with the other leg and arm. For more advanced exercises you can move your arm and leg out at a right angle from your body, keeping them above your spine, and hold them there for twenty seconds. Your stomach should be pulled in the entire time, supporting your lower back.

11: Superman

Strengthens lower back

Lie flat on your stomach, reaching your arms out in front of you with the palms down. Spread your extremities straight out in all four directions and lift your arms and legs simultaneously for enough repetitions to cause some mild fatigue. Continue to look down during the movement, and don't over-extend your neck up. This exercise is about how long you can make your body stretch — not how high you can get it. Focus on squeezing your butt as you lift. Try to make it to one min-ute.

12 (Stretch): The Seated Pretzel

Stretches lower-middle upper back and hip

Sit down with your legs stretched in front of you. Bring your right foot up and set it down on the outside of your left knee. For back support, put your right hand behind your right butt cheek. Bring your left toe straight up. Reach your left hand up as if in-dicating "stop" and drop your chin. Then twist to the right and bring your left triceps to the outside of the right thigh. To go deeper, twist more to apply pressure against your right thigh. Act like a string is pulling the top of your head up to elongate the spine. Breathe by expanding your rib cage like you are blowing up a balloon. Really concentrate on taking deep breaths every time.

Note for exercises 13 and 14: For all reclining abdominal exercises, keep your lower back flat on the ground. Pretend a quarter is trapped between the floor and your lower back, and keep your belly taut to train your stomach to be flat. As soon as you feel your lower back tenting up, stop and pull it back down as flat as possible before continuing. If this gets too hard, stop and hold it down as flat as possible for thirty seconds. Pretend there is a dumbbell tied to a string attached to your belly button, and it is pulling your stomach down toward the quarter.

13: Leg Drop

Strengthens entire abdominal area

Lie on your back with your hands on your chest and put your knees at a 45-degree angle and your feet in the air. Drop your heels down, tap the mat, and bring back up to 45 degrees. Do as many as you can (to failure). As soon as your lower back starts to arch up, return back to 45 degrees; keep pushing yourself a little bit further each time with your back glued to the quarter. Beginners, do one leg at a time. Advanced, do it with straight legs.

14: X Crunch

Strengthens upper abdominals

Lie on your back with your feet on the ground and your knees at a 45-degree angle. Cross your arms behind your head, putting your opposite hand to the opposite shoulder to form an X behind your head. Rest your head in this X and keep your neck loose (in the beginning, you can put a tennis ball under your chin as a reminder). Using your abdominal muscles, crunch up about 30 degrees from the floor. Without holding your breath, you need to suck in your belly button to the floor to tighten the natural girdle you have (it's a muscle called the transversus abdominis) to keep the entire six-pack tight.

Also pull up your pelvic muscles (like when you are holding in your pee) to strengthen the bottom of the natural girdle. Do as many as you can, looking up toward the ceiling the entire time. Then repeat Up, Dog, Up (exercise 9) to stretch your abdominals.

15: Seated Drop Kick

Strengthens quadriceps

Sit with your legs straight out in front of you. Bend your right leg up with the knee pointing toward the ceiling. To keep your back straight, interweave your hands around this knee. Act like there is a string pulling from the top of your head, elongating your spine (and don't bob your head). Lift your straight left leg six inches off the ground, keeping your left toe pointed toward the ceiling. Lift twenty-five times, then switch legs. Do each leg twice. The only body part that moves is the leg; for variation, lift leg and move side to side.

16: Invisible Chair

Strengthens entire leg

Sit in a chair position (with no chair!) with your back against a wall, and with your palms resting on your knees. Ideally, have a stool below you, so you can grab it or sit on it when you're done. Keep your heels directly below your knees and at a 90-degree angle; your relaxed shoulders should be rolled back and the back of your head should be against the wall. Hold for as long as you can, and try to work up to two minutes. Keep your face relaxed and breathe.

17 (Stretch): Nice Thighs

Stretches quadriceps

While standing on one leg, bend the knee of the opposite leg and grab the foot behind your back with interwoven fingers (or use one arm to hold something to keep balanced). Pull the foot toward your butt while lifting your chest forward and squeezing your shoulder blades together. Keep your knees together. Switch legs. Keep your abs pulled in the entire time, to support your lower back. Hold each for twenty seconds.

Mind

64. Get Rid of the Baggage

It takes a while for some people, but one of the tricks of a successful waist-management plan is letting go some of the negative emotions associated with dieting. Two strong emotions most associated with dieting:

Guilt: No matter what kind of diet you may have tried in the past, you've undoubtedly worked with a list of off-limits foods. High-protein diets might ban potatoes. Low-fat diets might ban cheese. Sugar-busting diets may ban you from ever setting foot in Aunt Thelma's kitchen again. Inevitably, like a child instructed not to touch the champagne flutes, you will want potatoes, you will want cheese, and you will find it incredibly rude to turn down Aunt Thelma's snickerdoodles three times in a row. So you cave. But because you've set yourself up with a list of banned foods, you perceive half a cookie, a hunk of Gouda, or three measly fries as first-degree diet homicide: The diet's dead. And that's where guilt sets in — from the fact that you know you deviated from a predetermined set of standards. That holds true for all levels of avoiders. We all identify with nutrition-induced guilt, and then we make a subconscious decision that it's easier to deal with the effects of being overweight than it is to feel the boulder-heavy guilt every time we want to smother a carrot in blue cheese.

Shame: For the person who feels he cheated on his diet — whether it was a simple kiss with a Kit Kat or an adulterous romp with a vat of cake batter — there's an even worse feeling than guilt. And that's the shame associated with dietary infidelity. You've cheated, so you now feel you lack the strength to succeed. So what are you going to tell your spouse and all your coworkers who've been watching you feast on iceberg lettuce at lunch for the past eight days? That, yes, you're a failure? That you could last on your diet for only a week? That you have one little thing you're doing and, by gosh, you can't even keep a stinking croissant out of your mouth? The public humiliation, or just the perceived threat of possible embarrassment, stems primarily from that societal disdain for obesity. This shame — a much more profound emotion than guilt — spins you back into the cycle of avoidance: It's better to not be on a diet and be fat, the avoider calculates, than to be on a diet and eventually prove to the world that you can't succeed.

So where does this leave us? Research actually shows that it's better for your health not to diet at all than to say you're dieting and steal spoonfuls of crème brûlée during every commercial break. That's because diets typically promote weight cycling and yo-yo dieting (gaining and losing, gaining and losing), which are actually more hazardous to your health than keeping a steady over-weight weight. (That's probably because most weight cyclers eventually gain back more than they lost and suffer the slings of shame.) So how does this all work for you, the person who knows she has to lose some weight but isn't necessarily breaking floorboards with every step? If you've spent years struggling with weight, it's likely you've experienced similar thoughts of guilt and shame and may even follow the same behavioral patterns. One of the strategies for bypassing the spiral of shame is to live and eat in the present, not being upset about what you ate in the past and not obsessing about what you'll eat in the future.

65. Use Mood Foods

When the brain chemicals associated with positive feelings (such as serotonin and dopamine) are in the up (or activated) position, you're chemically high. But when they're down, you experience a big emotional and chemical downfall. And this puts you in a state of anxiety that sends you searching for the foods, especially simple carbohydrates, that get you back to the chemical high. That's how illegal drugs work too; users keep seeking the high not always for its own sake but to avoid the lows. You're constantly fighting to get back to that place of neurochemical comfort. When these chemicals are high, your weight gets lower, and when they're lower, you reach for the foods that eventually make your weight higher.

66. Learn the Science to Making a Change

We all know that making a change in your life is as mental as it is behavioral. Research shows that this is the best four-step process for making change:

Be positive: It works for coaches, bosses, and parents, as well as waist managers. If you blame yourself for your weight, if you are depressed about your weight, if your mood is fouler than a subway station in August, then your first job is to refocus. You need to think about what you can do, how you can do it, why it's good for you, and how you'll succeed. In the weight-loss game, poker-faced confidence trumps negativity every time. By stripping yourself of the negative emotions of guilt and shame, you'll make the right rational (and long-term) decisions about your eating obstacles.

Add some support: You may not know it, but your world is full of saboteurs — people out to make you fatter than Microsoft's coffers. There's the boss who brings in sweets for every Thursday meeting. The friend who brings you a pie when you're upset. The spouse who suggests pitchers of margaritas and a plate of cheese nachos to celebrate the end of the week. Maybe there's nothing wrong with their intentions, but there is something wrong with the fact that their attempts to appeal to your heart are actually damaging it. What we want you to do — no, *need* you to do — is develop a support system of people who know your goals, know your obstacles, know your weaknesses, and know your strengths. (Don't have anyone? You can hook up on the Internet, at www.realage.com.) This person will be your sounding board, your comfort system, and your measure of accountability. With public accountability — that is, you reporting in on those daily struggles and successes — you're more likely to make a permanent change.

Make a gesture: Small gestures (ones not involving individual fingers flung at passing motorists) can be viewed as anything from signs of love to signs of bribery. Token gestures can also help kick-start the psychology of change. Just making a seemingly small change will help determine your long-term success, whether it's buying a pedometer, a health-club membership, or new walking shoes; throwing away the unhealthy foods in your pantry; and even setting up a computer file to record your progress. If you make one small move like this, research shows that you'll be three times more likely to follow through with the specific plan you intend to follow. This small change is your way of putting the key in your waist management ignition (www.sharecare.com can help).

Then do it: Once you start with the small gesture, you're ready. Eat a full day's worth of perfect-for-you food. Walk thirty minutes today, tomorrow, and every day after that. That's right, thirty minutes of walking a day is the minimum commitment. (You can break it up into smaller segments if you can't do it all at once.) Then make a second action commitment: Commit to doubling (or tripling) your daily vegetable intake. With one foot, take one specific first step. The other foot has no choice but to follow.

67. Excuse-Proof Your Life

When it comes to working out, most of us have two excuse cards we like to play: We have the ace of "no time" and the jack of "it's not convenient." Now, we know you're busy. We know you're juggling more balls than a twelve-armed clown. We know it's easier to sit on the couch than to do a push-up on the floor. But we also know this: Time and convenience aren't excuses. First of all, with this plan, you don't need a whole lot of time (thirty minutes a day to walk and thirty minutes a week to do some resistance training). If you don't have the time to do this, then you have to be willing to admit that the problem is not the fact that you're out of time but the fact that your life is so out of control that you can't budget enough time for your health and well-being. Plus, the newfound energy will enable you to do more than you could before. And second, you don't need a gym or fancy equipment; heck, it takes more time to drive to the gym and change clothes than it does to actually work out. You can do all of this activity at home — with a few modest pieces of equipment or even by making use of items you already have. In fact, in the YOU Workout, you use your body as your weights. It sure beats spending your workout time waiting at the exercise machine for someone to finish her issue of *Quilting Quarterly*. Yes, it's easy to say you're too tired, too stressed, too busy, too this, or too that. We say, too bad. The only way you'll strip away the fat is to start by stripping away the excuses.

68. Let Your Brain, Not Your Eyes, Decide Your Hunger

Clearly, some of us eat for physical reasons (we're hungry), and some of us gnaw on leftover Halloween candy for emotional reasons (we're steamed at the boss about having to start and finish a new report by 10 a.m., and it's 9:47). But sometimes it's not always easy to figure out the difference. To help, you need to start using the YOU Diet Hunger Test. Throughout the day, record your level of hunger as judged by this scale. Stay tuned to what your stomach is telling you, not what's happening outside with stresses (the car battery died), emotions (spouse is working late again), or habits (Conan equals bowl of Apple Jacks). This process will help you really feel your hunger, so that you can let your stomach, not your emotions, dictate your habits.

0 Tank = Hungry. It feels as if you haven't eaten since junior year of high school.

1/2 Tank = Edge is off. You're OK, not desperate, like maybe when you're driving home from work.

3/4 Tank = Satisfied and not hungry. You can go much longer without food. You just ate nuts and had a drink before dinner.

1 Full Tank = Full and comfortable. It's the way you feel after finishing an average-portion, healthful meal.

Overflow Level S = Stuffed. You could've stopped two scoops of pudding ago.

Overflow Level OS = Overstuffed. Audible groaning detected.

Overflow Level BP = Button Pop/Exploding. It's the typical Thanksgiving gorge. You feel sick and even take the name of your momma's stuffing in vain.

The way the test works is, every time you find yourself reaching for the cheese sauce or cookie box, rate your hunger. Then think about whether you're reaching for the leftover lasagna because you're truly hungry or for a reason that has absolutely nothing to do with hunger. Ideally, you'll want to stay in the Three-fourths to Full Tank range — satisfied at all times. And you'll get there by eating regularly throughout the day. (See 14-Day YOU: On a Diet Plan on page 199 for details.) After applying these gauges for two weeks, you'll start to instinctively know why you're eating, and, better, you'll train yourself to eat simply to keep your stomach satisfied — and not your emotions.

69. Ask Yourself, WHY?

The fact is, you *know*. You know if you need to lose weight. You can tell by the way you look, by the way you feel, and by whether your clothes feel tighter than an unopened pickle jar.

But to be able to make changes — sustainable changes — you not only have to know *what* you've done to your figure. You also have to know *why* you're abusing your body, in the form of the emotional and physical triggers that led you to gain waist. To start, perform a self-administered "why" test — that is, keep asking yourself "why" questions about your weight until you come to the real answer about why you want to lose weight and why you can't. It may go something like this:

Why do I want to lose weight? Because I want to fit into my old pair of jeans.

Why do I want to fit into my old pair of jeans? Because I'd have more confidence.

Why do I want more confidence? Because I'll feel better trying to meet new people.

Why do I want to meet new people? Because I'm recently divorced and hoping to start a new relationship.

Why do I want to start a new relationship? Because I'm feeling lonely . . . And that's likely to be where the thread of questions stops — where you can link the first question to the last answer. You want to lose weight because you're lonely, but the likely cause of your weight gain is the very same thing: that you're lonely.

70. Change the Power Structure in Your Relationship with Food
You know who holds all the cards

in your food-versus-you relationship? Yep. Tootsie Rolls. And whipped cream. And fried eggplant. And anything else that constantly tempts you and teases you. Without sounding too much like a wrestling ring announcer, it's time to take on these temptations and change the power structure in this relationship. C'mon, a bag of chips is stronger than you? The truth is that feeling powerless over food is a superficial emotion that actually covers up many other deeper ones that are really frustrating you — whether you're feeling unsure, unsafe, angry, or empty. The minute you cross the line between seeing food as a source of energy and seeing it as a security blanket, you're in deep trouble. Remember how hard it was to give up your blankie? By making yourself dependent on food for emotional support, rather than your relationships or your soul, you abdicate your power to control your eating. So we urge you to ask yourself some questions about your hunger: Do you demand immediate gratification from food because you are powerless in other parts of your life? Are you even aware of what you're eating, or is eating more like popping pain medication? The medical community can't concoct a magic bullet that dives into this deeper, emotional level of eating. And frankly, we're not even sure the words we (or anyone) say can inspire this change. This change is an internal one — but one that has some pretty major external benefits as well. When you feel powerless in all other aspects of your life, the only remaining area that remains in your control is how you put food into your mouth, so this is how you express your desire for power. That's why telling people not to eat removes their one remaining pillar of independence, so they rebel by eating even more. So what you need to start doing is seeking power in your life — whether it's through spirituality, work, or even relationships. That way, you take the power away from the knife and fork and put it back into your heart and soul.

71. Adopt the YOU-Turn Mantra

If you've ever ridden in a car with a GPS satellite navigation system, you know how it works. Plug in your destination, and the system — using satellites to plot your current and final points — tells you exactly what to do when. Turn left after 400 feet. Stay straight. Get in right lane. But let's say you make a mistake and miss a turn or turn onto the wrong street. The GPS doesn't berate you, doesn't scold you, doesn't tell you that you might as well drive off a cliff, since you made a mistake and missed First Avenue. Instead, all it says, very politely, is this: "At the next available moment, make an authorized U-turn." The GPS recognizes the mistake matter-of-factly and simply guides you back onto the right road. The GPS allows for mistakes and tries to help you correct them. That's the kind of mentality we want you to have. You're going to make wrong turns. You're going to turn left at the hot dogs, make a right at the blueberry pie, and occasionally merge onto the interstate of banana-nut pancakes with a side order of sausage patties. Does that mean you should steer off the dietary cliff and fall into the fatty crevasse of destructive eating? Of course not. What it means is that you need to pay closer attention to the road signs and the instructions about how to make it to your final destination. It also means that you can't beat yourself up with a basket of croissants every time you lick a little whipped cream off your finger. So what you're going to do — right now — is acknowledge that you will face obstacles. And instead of falling into the avoidant and defeatist mentality by drop-kicking healthy eating the moment you make one bad choice, you will confront it. How? By repeating the YOU Diet Mantra:

"At the next available moment, make

an authorized YOU-Turn."

"At the next available moment, make an authorized YOU-Turn."

"At the next available moment, make an authorized YOU-Turn."

Get back on the right road.

What kills any regimen of healthy eating isn't the occasional dessert or slice of pizza; it's the cascade of behavior that happens after the initial indulgence. Use this mantra to steer yourself back — to understand that you can make mistakes but that you can correct and overcome them with some nonjudgmental coaxing. Why does it work?

❑ It gives you a mental crutch to carry when you're faced with difficult eating situations.

❑ It reminds you to be confident,

to be positive, to know that the harm isn't in the first mistake, it's in not figuring out how to deal with it.

❑ It reinforces the grand scheme of this whole plan — the reason why you're trying to manage your waist.

The long-term benefits to your health far outweigh what you're giving up in your Pyrex dish.

72. Plan to Fail — and Develop Contingency Plans for When You Do

We keep tires in our trunks in case one goes flat. We keep candles in our drawers in case the power goes out. We keep backups of files in case our computers crash. (And some of us wish we backed them up more often.) And that's good; contingency plans give you the mental assurance that you'll be able to adapt to unexpected crises. But the one area where we don't make backup plans is in our diets. We eat broccoli, fish, and fruit for three days, then splurge on a double-fat burger with supersize fries on the fourth. For so many of us, that's grounds for euthanizing the diet right away — putting us right back in touch with our three favorite food groups of chocolate, chips, and chocolate chips. Instead, start carrying a dietary contingency plan — a diet emergency pack for those times when you may experience a crash-causing blowout in one of your meals. Follow this three-step contingency plan to help you cope with occasional mishaps and potential catastrophes. Exercise it the moment you feel you're deviating from your waist management plan:

❑ **Mental:** Say the YOU-Turn mantra ten times. Let the mantra remind you that it's OK to stray occasionally, that you can take control of the situation and steer yourself back, and that the positive reinforcement and confidence that come with overcoming challenges will give you the mental strength of a tank. Plus, the relaxing aspect of it will help influence your serotonin levels in your favor. And it will help distract you, which is what you need when you're beelining toward the bonbons.

❏ *Physical:* Do a yoga pose or try the hippie stretch (see the YOU Workout). We suggest the downward dog pose, balancing your weight on your hands and feet with your butt hiked toward the ceiling in an inverted V. Not only will it help you refocus, give you a few moments to take deep breaths, and remind you of your goals, but it will also work because it's sort of difficult to eat when you're upside down.

❏ *Nutritional:* Keep in your fridge a container of baby carrots, celery, or any crisp vegetable of your choice, or a favorite apple type (yes, types matter to our individual taste choices). Carrots and apples are perfect anti-stress foods because, one, they have just a tinge of sweetness to satisfy that craving, and, two, they give you something to crunch into at times when you really want to sink your teeth into your boss's neck. This will become your turn-to food — that is, the food you turn to when you feel angry, frustrated, mad, sad, or upset — as well as the one that will help you feel better about the nutritional mistakes you may have just made.

Lifestyle

73. Learn How Stress Makes You Fat

Along the intestinal freeway, the parking garage for fat that is your omentum looks like a stocking draped over a hanger (the stomach is the hanger), but changes depending on how many calories you're storing. In a person with little omentum fat, your stomach looks as if it has nylons hanging off it — thin, permeable, with some webbing. But in a person with a lot of omentum fat, the hanger looks as if snow pants are hanging on it — the fat globules are so fat that there's no netting or webbing whatsoever. (While cells can convert to fat in the liver, getting fatter is more a case of your existing cells growing. When you add body fat, you don't get more fat cells, just more fat in each cell.) Genetics certainly helps dictate whether you're going to have a big waist or a small one. But your lifestyle — in terms of stress — often plays a bigger role in deciding whether you'll have large amounts of belly fat or not. Here's how it works:

Historically, mankind has two types of stresses. The first kind is the immediate soil-your-loincloth stress (in other words, the dinner-seeking saber-toothed tiger is closing in fast). In that fight-or-flight scenario, your body produces the neurotransmitter norepinephrine to speed your heart rate, breathing, and 100-yard-dash time to the cave. When that happens, the last thing you're thinking about is grilling up some tubers on the campfire, so your hunger levels are squashed. That's because your body inhibits a chemical during periods of acute stress (it's why exercise cuts appetite, because your body senses that you're in acute stress). So high levels of stress work in favor of your waist: They take away your appetite and speed up your metabolism.

The second kind of stress that early man faced is the chronic struggle brought on by drought and famine. In contrast to the thirty or forty seconds they sweated over tiger fangs, our ancestors worried about survival all the time, and their bodies had to deal with chronic stress. When they faced famine, they sought out as many calories as they could, and their metabolism downshifted to help them conserve energy. The modern-day version of this problem is chronic stress, which makes us seek out calories and then downshifts our metabolism. Our bodies respond by storing the excess energy to call upon during periods where there may not be enough food. Those extra calories are stored in the omentum — our abdominal fat depot — to have on hand in case we are denied food. The liver, which is the relay station for energy circulation in the body, has immediate access to this omental fat, unlike the fat cluttering up the back of our thighs. When people are under stress, their bodies release high amounts of steroids into their bloodstream in the form of the hormone cortisol. In acute cases (the tiger or a car accident), steroids stick around briefly. But when you're under chronic stress (the drought or the nagging task), your body needs to find a way to deal with those high levels of cortisol. So your omentum clears the cortisol steroids; it has receptors that bind to them and can suck them out of the bloodstream.

Managing your waist size also comes down to also managing the stresses in your life.

74. Change the Environment, Not the Behavior

In previous diet attempts, you may have sworn to make all kinds of behavioral changes: Not gonna snack, not gonna have dessert, not gonna eat bread, not gonna eat after 9 p.m., not gonna eat out. That's all well and good, especially if you snack on chips, have chocolate death for dessert, and eat 8,000 calories at the Big Butt Buffet. The savvier approach, though, is to realize that some of our behavioral urges are indeed hardwired and trying to suppress them is a recipe for failure. Face it, we need to eat every few hours, and we do have dopamine receptors that cause us to crave certain foods, such as sweets. So what should you do? Don't fight your biology; rather, change the environment to make your biology work for you, not against you. In practical terms, that means you need to change your environment so you're less likely to be caught in a storm. Keep fruit in your pantry instead of chips. Meet your friends at a juice bar rather than a breakfast place known for its mile-high pancakes. You can't eat them if they're not on the menu. And when you eat out? Choose a fish place rather than a burger joint. What's so wrong with a wonderful piece of grilled mustard-crusted salmon and a side of steamed veggies with garlic? While there's nothing earth-shattering about snacking on fruit or ordering a lean piece of fish, the aha moment comes when you learn not to fight the wave, by denying yourself the pleasure of dining out, for example, but to ride the wave, by adjusting the environment to your behaviors. Fundamentally, you want to make it easier to do the right thing. Make the tough decisions when you are in a cold, calculating state rather than when you are in the heat of ravaging your pantry. Choose what you're going to eat in the supermarket — actually, before you go to the supermarket (make a list in advance, stick to it, and *never* shop on an empty stomach) — rather than when the fridge door is off its hinges as you scavenge for food. By planning ahead, instead of finding leftover cheesecake in there, you'll find a bunch of fresh grapes. And make a workout (such as ours below) so seamless to the flow of your life that all the usual excuses become even more embarrassing.

75. Choose Friends Wisely

If you socialize with the every-day-is-a-reason-to-eat-lasagna crowd, chances are you're going to be knee deep in ricotta without much chance of digging yourself out (except via fork). But if you're surrounding yourself with the let's-run-a-5K set, bingo, you're going to be spending more time running around the neighborhood and less time running to the convenience store. Does that mean we suggest you ditch any overweight friends? Of course not. But maybe it means you shouldn't schedule as many lunch dates with that person, or maybe you should become the ringleader to start a weekly hike along the local nature trail. Healthy living is as infectious as unhealthy living. And you can decide which bug you want to catch.

76. Go to Sleep
Getting enough sleep keeps you thin. That's because when your body doesn't

get the seven to eight hours of sleep it needs every night to get rejuvenated, the neurons in your brain don't secrete the normal amounts of serotonin or dopamine. To compensate, your body craves sugary foods that will give you an immediate release of serotonin and dopamine. Lack of sleep throws off your entire system and increases your appetite. Lack of sleep can become an even bigger factor as you age. When you get older, the pineal gland in your brain produces less of the sleep hormone melatonin, resulting in a craving for carbohydrates.

77. Get Close

Both on a physical level and on a psychological level, seek out positive interactions with other people. Evidence shows that increased amounts of oxytocin may decrease blood pressure and lower the effects of stress and control your appetite. If nothing else, it's a darn good reason to schedule a weekly massage. And it may help explain why things such as meditation and hypnosis — which are suspected to increase oxytocin levels — can be helpful with weight loss. Also, while there's as much information on this as on obesity in elite marathoners, the fear of touch and lack of oxytocin release may be one reason why abused individuals often have problems with waist management.

78. Have More Sex

In any waist management plan, you can stay satisfied. Not in the form of a dripping double cheeseburger but in the form of safe, healthy, monogamous sex. Some have observed that having healthy sex could help you control your food intake; by satisfying one appetite center, you seem to satisfy the other.

79. Talk to Your Doc About Reinforcements

When you start your diet, schedule an appointment with your doc when you're likely to hit the hump — about day thirty. You may be a candidate for Wellbutrin. The drug is thought to work by helping emotional eaters decrease cravings. The reason why it works: It helps us not think and obsess over food. It can program our bodies to get back into our natural position — that is, not substituting a six-pack of Hershey bars for a spouse who doesn't listen, a boss who doesn't understand, or a child who feels like rolling soup cans down the aisle. Very soon, more and more new classes of drugs will be developed to help curb cravings and appetites, and they're worth exploring with your doctor. But these are short-term boosters to help you along your path.

80. Get Up

One unsung form of exercise: fidgeting. Studies show that fidgety people are simply skinnier people. If you have two people working the same job and eating the same diet, the one who gets up to talk to someone down the hall rather than emailing her will be skinnier. Studies show that it isn't some mysterious food, organ, cell, or gremlin that makes these people burn up fat like an iron skillet, it's these fidgeting movements. Now, that's not to say that if you go on an all-fidgeting, leg-shaking, finger-tapping program (think Robin Williams), you'll be thinner than a Hilton sister. But numerous studies have shown that the more you move — in very subtle ways — the more calories your body will burn throughout the day. Find an excuse to move your muscles wherever you are. Clear the dishes. Stand up and walk in circles while you're on the phone. Walk down the hall to ask a coworker a question, rather then IM-ing her. Sit on an exercise ball for the first hour you work on your computer (a great core strengthener). Tap your toes in a meeting. Take every opportunity to move around, and you'll give your body subtle metabolism boosters that may just have more-than-subtle effects.

81. Keep Your Hands Full

You'd think that being plopped in front of a TV playing Xbox would mean that you're destined for a life of fatness. But that's not the case; studies show that playing video games is actually not correlated with obesity. Why? Turns out that when you've got your two hands on the controllers and your fingers moving faster than Liberace's, that means one thing: Your paws won't be knuckle-deep in a bowl of chocolate-covered raisins. (Some games even have foot mats for you to make commands with your feet too, so you can get a complete workout; ask your kids about the Dance Dance Revolution craze. Wii Fit works too if you don't take too many breaks.) Now,

that's not to say that an intimate relationship with Super Mario should be
your number one strategy, but it does
prove an underlying point. When
you keep your hands and brain oc-
cupied — whether with video games,
gardening, or removing a spleen — it
means you're putting your brain into
the state you want: not thinking about
eating and not automatically reaching
for something to put in your mouth.

82. Breathe Deep
If you can take long, deep breaths
through your nose, you'll stimulate
a short-lived gas called nitric oxide,
which opens up your arteries and
relaxes you. That can help keep you
calm when you're facing tough emotional situations. Inhale a deep, long
breath. Then, to exhale, suck your

belly button toward your spine to push the diaphragm up and empty all the air from your lungs.

83. Research Complementary Methods

The following supplements have been shown to have effectiveness in some aspect of waist management: chromium picolinate, grapefruit oil, African mango, Garcinia, Hoodia, 5-HTP, L-carnitine, coenzyme Q10, turmeric, jojoba beans, simmondsin (see www.360-5.com for a debate about the pros and cons of many of these). Consult your doctor about which ones may be appropriate for you.

84. Maintain Energy Levels

Our circadian rhythm means we're

hardwired to have an energy dip between 1 p.m. and 4 p.m. (though no
one knows why evolution thought
that was a good idea). Taking a nap
makes lots of sense but can be difficult to accomplish if you want to keep
your job. Fortunately, you can at least
compensate for it — and likely lessen
it — with these strategies:

❑ *Make every meal count.* You
   can't just blame lunch for heavy
   afternoon eyelids — the post-
   lunch dip can even hit people
   who skip that meal. Your energy level is affected by what
   you do or don't eat the whole
   day long — try to eat no foods
   with added sugars or syrups
   and no grain that is less than
   100 percent whole — this keeps

your blood sugar more constant and you more alert.

❑ *Try a little caffeine.* We said a *little*. It helps you sustain afternoon attention, but beware — it also might keep you from going to bed on time, creating an even worse dip tomorrow (morning).

❑ *Take a hike.* Or just walk to lunch the long way. People in one study felt less afternoon fatigue on days when they worked out during lunch. Regular activity is key; one workout on one drowsy day won't give you afternoon energy all month.

85. Get the Whole Family Involved

In this era of soccer games, dance recitals, Mom working late, sister having a science project, and brother putting together a PowerPoint, it's easy to fall into the trap: Eat quick, eat in front of the TV, eat junk. Big mistake. Of all the things you can do to influence the health of your child, perhaps the most important is to make family dinner a priority. Research shows that having family dinner more than twice a week can positively influence a child's waist, eating behavior, and overall psychological development. If you want to teach your whole family about eating right, try these strategies:

Play Red Light, Green Light: Kids love this game on the playground, but you can also play it in the kitchen to teach young kids about healthy foods. For young kids, make a short list of green-light "yes" foods (such as vegetables, fruit, nonfried fish), red-light "no" foods (such as soda), and yellow-light "treat" foods (the 100 percent whole grain, 100 percent omega-3 chia muffin or Lifestyle 180 bar — see *YOU: On a Diet,* revised edition, for this recipe — after dinner). It makes it fun for kids and teaches them principles that will last. Other cool games that work well with some kids:

❑ Find the best cereal in the store (based on what you learn from labels; see below).

❑ Have a kids cooking day (pick one healthy meal that your kids could assist you with).

❑ Toss out the junk at a friend's

house (with said friend's approval).

Create a mantra: Kids can be motivated to change their behavior if you introduce a fun system that gets their little imaginative and competitive minds churning. One we love: The "5 to 0 Go!" system developed by the Cleveland Clinic. Basically, you come up with a daily checklist of 5 things you need to eat or do every day, 4 things, 3 things, and so on. Throughout the day, you track what they've done to meet the goals, and you can even make it a daily competition between siblings. Here's an example:

- ❏ 5 veggies/fruits
- ❏ 4 servings of nonfat dairy (for

calcium and vitamin D3)
- ❑ 3 compliments (create a positive environment)
- ❑ 2 or fewer hours of screen time
- ❑ 1 hour or more of play/exercise

MORE

86. Know Your Fighting Weight

In all likelihood, the most common way you've measured your so-called dietary success or failure is by pounds lost. If you've lost down to your target weight, then you've won. If not, you've lost. But the reality is that over the long term, all of us will intermittently gain and lose small amounts of weight, even when we're trying to lose it. For one, our water weight often fluctuates depending on what we're eating. The reason why so many low-carb dieters lose weight fast is because the lack of carbohydrates causes them to lose glycogen stores from their muscles, and with this loss of glycogen comes a loss of a lot of water; as soon as they reinstate the carbs, the glycogen comes back to the muscles and attracts the water. That adds the pounds right back. So the first 5 to 11 pounds of weight loss on a low-carb diet is the fake loss due to a temporary loss of water. Instead of tracking your weight by a single goal weight of, say, 145 pounds, what you're going to do is pick your weight class. You're going to pick a range of weight that's comfortable for you — say, 142 to 148 pounds (or 31 inches to 33 inches of waist size). When you divulge your weight to someone (not that anyone will be asking), it should never be in one number; you need to think of your weight as an ideal range. For one thing, this allows for the natural fluctuations that occur. For another, it also does something even more crucial to your psychological success: It stops you from focusing on some arbitrary number that promotes the idea of all-or-nothing success or failure. And it puts your mind in the right programming mode — to remind yourself that your body is supposed to change.

87. Have Regular Readings

Not just with your book club or by an astrologer. These regular readings are about tracking your health numbers. Instead of measuring your success through the scale, the real measurement — and test — of your success is seeing whether you are alive and vibrant, and if so, reduce your cardiovascular risk, as evidenced in the following test readings:

Blood pressure: Optimum level is 115/76. Blood pressure readings can be variable, so have your BP taken in the morning, during the day, and at night, as part of your normal activities (except for thirty minutes after exercise, when it will naturally be higher). Take the average of three readings to come up with your base number. After that, take readings every month to help you monitor your progress. (If your BP is high, then you can track it daily.)

Lipid profile blood test: Have one now to establish your baseline measurement, then have your blood analyzed every other year so that you and your doctor can watch changes and make appropriate adjustments to your eating and/or drug plan.

HDL (healthy) cholesterol: You're at low risk if your HDL is greater than 50 mg/dl. But like basketball players, the higher the better. In fact, if your HDL is over 100 mg/dl (active, not fake HDL), the chances of having a heart attack or stroke related to lack of blood flow are smaller than the chance that a Hollywood celeb could walk through Boise unnoticed. (Except in some extremely rare cases where HDL malfunctions inside the body, there has never been a heart attack or stroke due to lack of blood flow reported in the entire medical literature in a person with a functional HDL over 100.)

LDL (lousy) cholesterol: You're at a low risk if your LDL is less than 100 mg/dl. By the way, research shows that for all women, and for men over sixty-five years old, the LDL and the HDL numbers are nearly equal in importance. So women and men over sixty-five don't need to obsess too much over LDL levels unless their HDL levels are too low.

Fasting blood sugar: Below 100 mg/dl.

C- reactive protein (highly sensitive): Below 1 mg/dl.

88. Explore Hidden Causes of Fat

You're doing everything right, yet your waist keeps expanding faster than a marshmallow in a microwave oven. The trouble might be your hormones:

1. ***Thyroid levels.*** Hypothyroidism slows down your metabolism like a tricycle slows down speed compared to Lance Armstrong on a racing bike. You can't burn calories like you used to.

2. ***PCOS, or polycystic ovarian syndrome.*** This accounts for unexplained weight gain in 20 percent of women. It's insulin resistance caused by abnormal secretion of a hormone by your darned ovaries.

3. ***Testosterone drops.*** These can occur in older men and post-menopausal women if you gain belly fat, because belly fat converts testosterone to estrogen.

Some say that's why fat single men hang out with guys and drink beer in bars — no libido and no aggressiveness even to try a line on a woman. But women with belly fat develop the problem too, as testosterone from their adrenals is a leading stimulator of libido. And less testosterone means less muscle mass, which makes it harder to burn fat (leading to weight gain). The cure: resistance exercise. The sign your testosterone levels are dropping: if you have to shave less often than you used to.

4. *Growth hormone dips.* This can decrease as you age when you don't sleep at least ninety minutes at a time because you have to get up to pee, leading to weight

gain. The best way to boost it naturally: get the right amount of sleep and exercise.

89. Remember Your Ancestry

Some people say their family has big bones or big cells. Some say their family has big appetites. Some say their family just has big beer coolers. If you gained weight as an adult, you can get a relatively accurate picture of what your ideal size should be by thinking about what you looked like when you were eighteen (for women) or twenty-one (for men); a time when you were at your metabolically most efficient and when you weren't stapled to an office chair for sixty hours a week. Most people gain their weight between the ages of twenty-one and sixty, so by looking at your size at eighteen or twenty-one, you'll have a good, though not quite scientific, idea of your factory settings. (If you're over forty; with today's adolescent obesity, such comparisons may not work in the future.) It's not perfect, but it's a thumbnail sketch of where you want to be. You can record your waist size (or closest guess) from when you were eighteen, but, more important, think about your shape. Ask your parents about their body sizes — or find pictures of them — when they were eighteen, to help give you a good idea of what you're supposed to look like.

90. Get Out and Just Play

Buy some balls, go outside, run, run, run. We've gotten so far away from the days when kids would play for hours outside, and we need to get some of that back — as adults too! There are many creative ways to get your activity. Go out and have fun.

91. Stop Beating Yourself Up

Somewhere and sometime, you've been led to believe that the only way you can lose weight is to eat perfectly all the time. That's not realistic. That's not fair. And that's why almost all diets fail. Perfection is impossible. We want you to focus on eating well most of the time — and not derailing all of your efforts every time you go a little bit off track.

92. to 98. Do the 7-Day *YOU: On a Diet* Plan

Besides eating meals with lean protein, healthy fats, and whole-grain carbohydrates (see some of our recipes here and online at www .realage.com and www.doctoroz. com), use this 7-day starter plan to get your body, your mind, and your kitchen all heading in the right direction.

Day 1: Saturday

1. **Walk:** Thirty minutes. Walking — whether you do it by yourself, with a friend, with your dog (only actual walking time counts, not time spent waiting for the dog to sniff), or around the dining room table — gives you your first dose of physical success. Walk every day for thirty minutes, and you'll establish the behavioral and motivational foundation for the YOU Diet.

2. **Stretch:** Do three to five minutes

of stretching after your walk. While stretching keeps your muscles limber and flexible to help prevent injury, it also has a meditative element to it, helping you refocus and cope with cravings. "No pain, no gain" does not apply here.

3. ***Dump your fridge:*** To make room for all the new, good food you're about to buy, it's time to rid your kitchen of the nutritional felons. The appeals are up; it's execution time. Read the label of everything in your kitchen cupboards, your refrigerator, your secret boxes, and everywhere else you stash food. If something has any of the following in one of the first five ingredients, throw it out. This is the *YOU: On a Diet* Rule of 5.

Don't have any of these five ingredients in the first five ingredients on the label:

❑ *Simple sugars and syrups:* This includes brown sugar, dextrose, corn sweetener, fructose (as in high-fructose corn syrup), glucose, corn syrup, honey, invert sugar, maltose, lactose, malt syrup, molasses, raw sugar, and sucrose. Keep a little table sugar handy, and honey, and maple sugar, because you'll use some for recipes.

❑ *Saturated fat:* This includes most four-legged animal fat, milk fat, butter or lard, and tropical oils, such as palm and coconut.

❑ *Trans fat:* This includes partially hydrogenated fats, vegetable oil blends that are hydrogenated, and many margarines and cooking blends. (If you must, use cholesterol-fighting sterol spreads such as Promise and Benecol.)

❑ *Enriched flours and all flours other than 100 percent whole grain or 100 percent whole wheat:* This includes enriched white flour, semolina, durum wheat, and any of the acronyms for flour that is not whole wheat — they should not be in your kitchen.

4. *Go food shopping:* Your current kitchen is most likely like a prison — it's filled with a lot of bad dudes. We want to turn your

kitchen into a nutritional honor society, so that it's filled with good-for-your-waist foods that make it easy (and automatic!) to eat right.

Day 2: Sunday

1. **Walk:** Thirty minutes.
2. **Stretch:** Do five minutes of stretching.
3. **Partner up:** If you try to undertake this alone, there's a much higher risk that you'll end up lips-first in a bowl of creamed corn. Find your YOU partner — be it a spouse, a friend, a co-worker — someone you can talk to about your goals, your meals, your new plan. Make a plan to talk (or email) five minutes every day — to tell him or her that you

walked that day and to itemize your day's meals. If you prefer a cyber friend, log on to www. realage.com and match up with a partner there. Better yet, try to find a partner or partners who are in this *with* you, on the same journey to good health. Share this book; share the knowledge you've learned; embark on a "work smart, not hard" journey together. It's one thing to lose three, four, or five inches yourself, but quite another when you can help contribute to America's collective loss in waistband size. After all, what's better than experiencing the satisfaction of helping yourself achieve your goal? Helping others do the same.

Day 3: Monday

1. **Walk:** Thirty minutes.
2. **Do the YOU Workout:** Follow the twenty-minute no-weights YOU Workout. Strength training helps you add muscle, which will help speed your metabolism and burn fat. Also start tightening your abs when you walk, which will help improve your posture and make your clothes fit better. Walk at a pace that raises your heart rate, or include twenty minutes of another cardiovascular exercise.
3. **Write it down (or type it in):** Generally, we're into guilt trips as much as we're into bourbon as a topical anesthetic, but we also think there's a fine line between guilt and motivation. One of the ways you can help reprogram

yourself is by writing down (or recording, for you technophiles) everything that you eat. In a way, it holds you accountable; you won't want to eat bad foods, because you won't want the visual reminder that you ate them. For these two weeks only — just to establish your new routine — write down *everything* you eat. Yep, even the three M&M's you just swiped. (For the technically savvy, some handheld devices have programs that allow you to scan the bar codes of the foods you eat. You enter the quantity you eat, and the program will keep track of your calories — see www.sharecare.com.)

4. **Go shopping:** With three days of walking under your soon-to-

be-loose belt, it's time you made another trip to the store. This time, make it the sports store — for a good pair of running shoes. Use them for walking only. Running shoes are lightweight, and they provide lots of heel cushioning (because they're made for people who pound the ground with more force). Your best bet: Go to a running specialty store, where the staff can not only measure your feet but analyze your stride and determine what kind of walker you are. (Note: Go shopping in the late afternoon when your feet are more likely to be swollen, to ensure the best fit.) If you like, you can also add these to your list:

❑ Socks with extra padding on the bottom. (Avoid cotton; you need socks that wick moisture away from your feet.)

❑ A yoga mat, so you don't slip and slide while enjoying the deep poses (and dumbbells or resistance bands if you're already advanced enough to use those).

Day 4: Tuesday

1. **Walk:** Thirty minutes.
2. **Stretch:** Do five minutes of stretching.
3. **Make any needed YOU-Turn:** It's not uncommon at this point for you to have already dabbled in the neighbor's cake, picked at the kids' chips, or snuck a few bites of a butter-covered pretzel from

the mall. And that's OK. Just get yourself back together. At the next available moment, make an authorized YOU-Turn. The next time you find yourself dancing with the Devil Dog, try these coping strategies:

❑ *The Lip Lick.* Breathe in, lick your lips, swallow, and breathe out slowly, saying "ohm." Let the cool air flow across your lips. The soothing move — which takes all of about three seconds — helps you to reset, calm down, and refocus.

❑ *The Waist Hang.* Stand up straight, bend over at your waist, and let your lower back relax. Reach for the floor, grab your elbows, or hold the back of your knees. The important thing is to let all of the tension you have stored in your back and hips unwind. Relax your neck completely. If you feel tight, don't straighten your knees.

Day 5: Wednesday

1 **Walk:** Thirty minutes.
2. **Do the YOU Workout:** Follow the twenty-minute no-weights YOU Workout.
3. **Call your doctor:** Remember, waist management is a team game, and your doctor is one of your MVPs. So schedule an appointment for thirty days from now (or sooner if you have a great relationship). You can use him or her to help you in many different ways:

❏ Update your vitals such as blood pressure, waist size, and heart rate. If you need a baseline for such numbers as HDL and LDL cholesterol (HDL is as important for women and men over sixty), now's a good time to schedule a physical, get a few blood tests, and talk to your doctor about your new plan.

❏ Having a physical will also prove helpful when you reach a plateau — when your waist and weight loss will seem to have stalled.

Day 6: Thursday

1. **Walk:** Thirty minutes.
2. **Stretch:** Do five minutes of stretching.
3. **Do a little bragging:** If you go

public with your success, it makes turning back more difficult. Tell a friend or a coworker about the progress you've made and the changes you've noticed.

Day 7: Friday

1. **Walk:** Thirty minutes.
2. **Do the YOU Workout:** Follow the twenty-minute no-weights YOU Workout.
3. **Restock your kitchen:** Check your pantry for ingredients you've run out of and make a shopping list for next week's recipes.
4. **Grade yourself:** Whether it's with work or a first date, it's always nice to have some way to know how you're progressing. Now is the time to take your waist measurement and weigh yourself, just

to see what changes you've made. In your first week, you may see up to a 1-inch waist reduction and a 2- to 4-pound weight reduction. You might even be able to drop one clothing size.

99. Enjoy the New YOU

Employ some, many, or all of our tips and you'll start to see — and feel — your body changing. Our mantra has always been: Diet Smart, Not Hard. We want healthy choices to become automatic — and fun — so that you can enjoy all of the wonderful things that life has to offer.

14-Day YOU: On a Diet Plan

This 14-day plan will help get you in the healthy-eating frame of mind, leaving you satisfied — with both your taste and the results. We believe that the best way to stick to a healthy plan is to automate some of your meals — that is, pick a favorite one or two things for breakfast or lunch and stick to them the majority of the time. That takes away the guesswork — and the temptations. Use our charts to help you choose a breakfast, lunch, and snack that you like. You can also sub in recipes you find in this book as well as more than 100 recipes found in the full version of *YOU: On a Diet,* revised edition.

DAY ONE

YOUR Breakfast Choices

For Cereal Lovers

Cooked oat cereal with 4 ounces of skim milk, or soy milk fortified with vitamin D and calcium, and 1 fistful of your favorite fruit

OR

1 cup Kashi high-fiber or cold-oat cereal (like plain Cheerios) with 1 fistful of your favorite fruit, with 4 ounces of skim milk, or soy milk fortified with vitamin D and calcium

For Egg Lovers

Egg-white omelet (3 egg whites and 1 whole egg), plus cut-up mixed veggies

OR

2 scrambled, poached, or hard-boiled eggs with 2 pieces of lean turkey sausage or tofu sausage (scramble with a little canola Pam spray, not butter)

For Bread Lovers

1 slice toasted 100% whole wheat bread with 1 teaspoon peanut butter, or 1 teaspoon apple or walnut butter or avocado spread

For Breakfast Haters

Magical Breakfast Blaster (see recipe, page 63)

YOUR Lunch Choices

Meal-Size Salad

Chopped salad: 6 chopped walnuts, chopped veggies (your choice), and chopped mixed greens tossed with 4 ounces of salmon, turkey, or chicken breast; with balsamic vinegar (2 parts) and olive oil (1 part) dressing

Soup and Salad

1 cup of Garden Harvest Soup (page 67) or Lisa's Great Gazpacho (page 68) and small chopped salad with veggies or a non-Caesar salad using olive or canola oil, or balsamic vinegar and olive oil dressing

Healthy Burger

Veggie burger or Boca Spicy Chik'n Patty on a toasted whole wheat English muffin with 1 tablespoon of fructose-free olive oil–based marinara sauce, sliced tomato, romaine lettuce or spinach leaves, plus slices of red onion

YOUR Morning and Afternoon Snack Choices

Fruit and Nuts

1/2 ounce raw nuts with an apple, banana, plum, pear, orange, wedge of melon, cup of berries, 2 kiwis, 1/2 grapefruit, or any other fruit

Grains and Berries

1/2 cup whole grain cereal mixed with 1/4 cup almonds and 1/4 cup dried berries, apricots, or raisins

Revved-up Veggies

1 cup of cut-up sautéed veggies, warmed in microwave and stuffed into small whole wheat pita

OR

Cut-up veggies dipped into 4 ounces plain, low-fat, no-sugar-added yogurt or low-fat cottage cheese mixed with lots of dill, chives, ginger, red pepper flakes, or other spices (your choice)

OR

Just plain cut-up veggies

Fruit and Yogurt

Low-fat probiotic (live culture) yogurt covered with 1/2 cup of canned, unsweetened peaches or mandarin oranges and some raisins

YOUR Dessert Choices

Eat Every Other Day

Sliced Peaches with Raspberries, Blueberries, and Chocolate Chips (page 75)

OR

1 ounce of dark chocolate (made with real cocoa), approximately three or four bites

YOUR Dinner Choices

(But Don't Eat After 8:30 p.m.)

Use a small plate covered with vegetables (sautéed in olive oil), with lean protein like turkey, chicken, or salmon, with 100-percent whole-grain pasta or rice

YOUR Drink Choices

Plain or sparkling water (with fruit slice if desired), skim milk, coffee, hot or iced tea (decaffeinated is best if you have problems sleeping), diet soda (but only 1 to 2 a day)

For breakfast, you may include an 8-ounce glass of fruit or vegetable juice, such as tomato juice or 100 percent grapefruit juice or orange juice with pulp, fortified with calcium and vitamin D

For dinner, you can include one glass of alcohol, which we prefer you to drink toward the end of the meal so it does not hinder your satiety center's ability to slow your voracious appetite. If you're a nondrinker, it's OK to swap for a teetotaler's cocktail made with low-sugar grape juice, sparkling water, and lime

DAY TWO

YOUR Breakfast Choices

For Cereal Lovers

Cooked oat cereal with 4 ounces of skim milk, or soy milk fortified with vitamin D and calcium, and 1 fistful of your favorite fruit

OR

1 cup Kashi high-fiber or cold-oat cereal (like plain Cheerios) with 1 fistful of your favorite fruit, with 4 ounces of skim milk, or soy milk fortified with vitamin D and calcium

For Egg Lovers

Egg-white omelet (3 egg whites and 1 whole egg), plus cut-up mixed veggies

OR

2 scrambled, poached, or hard-boiled eggs with 2 pieces of lean turkey sausage or tofu sausage (scramble with a little canola Pam spray, not butter)

For Bread Lovers

1 slice toasted 100% whole wheat bread with 1 teaspoon peanut butter, or 1 teaspoon apple or walnut butter or avocado spread

For Breakfast Haters

Magical Breakfast Blaster (see recipe, page 63)

YOUR Lunch Choices

Meal-Size Salad

Chopped salad: 6 chopped walnuts, chopped veggies (your choice), and chopped mixed greens tossed with 4 ounces of salmon, turkey, or chicken breast; with balsamic vinegar (2 parts) and olive oil (1 part) dressing

Soup and Salad

1 cup of Garden Harvest Soup (page 67) or Lisa's Great Gazpacho (page 68) and small chopped salad with veggies or a non-Caesar salad using olive or canola oil, or balsamic vinegar and olive oil dressing

Healthy Burger

Veggie burger or Boca Spicy Chik'n Patty on a toasted whole wheat English muffin with 1 tablespoon of fructose-free olive oil–based marinara sauce, sliced tomato, romaine lettuce or spinach leaves, plus slices of red onion

YOUR Morning and Afternoon Snack Choices

Fruit and Nuts

1/2 ounce raw nuts with an apple, banana, plum, pear, orange, wedge of melon, cup of berries, 2 kiwis, 1/2 grapefruit, or any other fruit

Grains and Berries

1/2 cup whole grain cereal mixed with 1/4 cup almonds and 1/4 cup dried berries, apricots, or raisins

Revved-up Veggies

1 cup of cut-up sautéed veggies, warmed in microwave and stuffed into small whole wheat pita

OR

Cut-up veggies dipped into 4 ounces plain, low-fat, no-sugar-added yogurt or low-fat cottage cheese mixed with lots of dill, chives, ginger, red pepper flakes, or other spices (your choice)

OR

Just plain cut-up veggies

Fruit and Yogurt

Low-fat probiotic (live culture) yogurt covered with 1/2 cup of canned, unsweetened peaches or mandarin oranges and some raisins

YOUR Dessert Choices

Eat Every Other Day

Sliced Peaches with Raspberries, Blueberries, and Chocolate Chips (page 75)

OR

1 ounce of dark chocolate (made with real cocoa), approximately three or four bites

YOUR Dinner Choices

(But Don't Eat After 8:30 p.m.)

Spicy Chili (page 72)

YOUR Drink Choices

Plain or sparkling water (with fruit slice if desired), skim milk, coffee, hot or iced tea (decaffeinated is best if you have problems sleeping), diet soda (but only 1 to 2 a day)

For breakfast, you may include an 8-ounce glass of fruit or vegetable juice, such as tomato juice or 100 percent grapefruit juice or orange juice with pulp, fortified with calcium and vitamin D

For dinner, you can include one glass of alcohol, which we prefer you to drink toward the end of the meal so it does not hinder your satiety center's ability to slow your voracious appetite. If you're a nondrinker, it's OK to swap for a teetotaler's cocktail made with low-sugar grape juice, sparkling water, and lime

DAY THREE

YOUR Breakfast Choices

For Cereal Lovers

Cooked oat cereal with 4 ounces of skim milk, or soy milk fortified with vitamin D and calcium, and 1 fistful of your favorite fruit

OR

1 cup Kashi high-fiber or cold-oat cereal (like plain Cheerios) with 1 fistful of your favorite fruit, with 4 ounces of skim milk, or soy milk fortified with vitamin D and calcium

For Egg Lovers

Egg-white omelet (3 egg whites and 1 whole egg), plus cut-up mixed veggies

OR

2 scrambled, poached, or hard-boiled eggs with 2 pieces of lean turkey sausage or tofu sausage (scramble with a little canola Pam spray, not butter)

For Bread Lovers

1 slice toasted 100% whole wheat bread with 1 teaspoon peanut butter, or 1 teaspoon apple or walnut butter or avocado spread

For Breakfast Haters

Magical Breakfast Blaster (see recipe, page 63)

YOUR Lunch Choices

Meal-Size Salad

Chopped salad: 6 chopped walnuts, chopped veggies (your choice), and chopped mixed greens tossed with 4 ounces of salmon, turkey, or chicken breast; with balsamic vinegar (2 parts) and olive oil (1 part) dressing

Soup and Salad

1 cup of Garden Harvest Soup (page 67) or Lisa's Great Gazpacho (page 68) and small chopped salad with veggies or a non-

Caesar salad using olive or canola oil, or balsamic vinegar and olive oil dressing

Healthy Burger

Veggie burger or Boca Spicy Chik'n Patty on a toasted whole wheat English muffin with 1 tablespoon of fructose-free olive oil–based marinara sauce, sliced tomato, romaine lettuce or spinach leaves, plus slices of red onion

YOUR Morning and Afternoon Snack Choices

Fruit and Nuts

1/2 ounce raw nuts with an apple, banana, plum, pear, orange, wedge of melon, cup of berries, 2 kiwis, 1/2 grapefruit, or any other fruit

Grains and Berries

1/2 cup whole grain cereal mixed with 1/4 cup almonds and 1/4 cup dried berries, apricots, or raisins

Revved-up Veggies

1 cup of cut-up sautéed veggies, warmed in microwave and stuffed into small whole wheat pita

OR

Cut-up veggies dipped into 4 ounces plain, low-fat, no-sugar-added yogurt or low-fat cottage cheese mixed with lots of dill, chives, ginger, red pepper flakes, or other spices (your choice)

OR

Just plain cut-up veggies

Fruit and Yogurt

Low-fat probiotic (live culture) yogurt covered with 1/2 cup canned, unsweetened peaches or mandarin oranges and some raisins or Lifestyle 180 Vita-Mix Green Smoothie, with psyllium husks added (page 66)

YOUR Dessert Choices

Eat Every Other Day

Sliced Peaches with Raspberries, Blueberries, and Chocolate Chips (page 75)

OR

1 ounce of dark chocolate (made with real cocoa), approximately three or four bites

YOUR Dinner Choices

(But Don't Eat After 8:30 p.m.)

Spicy Chili leftovers

YOUR Drink Choices

Plain or sparkling water (with fruit slice if desired), skim milk, coffee, hot or iced tea (decaffeinated is best if you have problems sleeping), diet soda (but only 1 to 2 a day)

For breakfast, you may include an 8-ounce glass of fruit or vegetable juice, such as tomato juice or 100 percent grapefruit juice or orange juice with pulp, fortified with calcium and vitamin D

For dinner, you can include one glass of alcohol, which we prefer you to drink toward the end of the meal so it does not hinder your satiety center's ability to slow your voracious appetite. If you're a nondrinker, it's OK to swap for a teetotaler's cocktail made with low-sugar grape juice, sparkling water, and lime

DAY FOUR

YOUR Breakfast Choices

For Cereal Lovers

Cooked oat cereal with 4 ounces of skim milk, or soy milk fortified with vitamin D and calcium, and 1 fistful of your favorite fruit

OR

1 cup Kashi high-fiber or cold-oat cereal (like plain Cheerios) with 1 fistful of your fa-

vorite fruit, with 4 ounces of skim milk, or soy milk fortified with vitamin D and calcium

For Egg Lovers

Egg-white omelet (3 egg whites and 1 whole egg), plus cut-up mixed veggies

OR

2 scrambled, poached, or hard-boiled eggs with 2 pieces of lean turkey sausage or tofu sausage (scramble with a little canola Pam spray, not butter)

For Bread Lovers

1 slice toasted 100% whole wheat bread with 1 teaspoon peanut butter, or 1 teaspoon apple or walnut butter or avocado spread

For Breakfast Haters

Magical Breakfast Blaster (see recipe, page 63)

YOUR Lunch Choices

Meal-Size Salad

Chopped salad: 6 chopped walnuts, chopped veggies (your choice), and chopped mixed greens tossed with 4 ounces of salmon, turkey, or chicken breast; with balsamic vinegar (2 parts) and olive oil (1 part) dressing

Soup and Salad

1 cup of Garden Harvest Soup (page 67) or Lisa's Great Gazpacho (page 68) and small chopped salad with veggies or a non-Caesar salad using olive or canola oil, or balsamic vinegar and olive oil dressing

Healthy Burger

Veggie burger or Boca Spicy Chik'n Patty on a toasted whole wheat English muffin with 1 tablespoon of fructose-free olive oil–based marinara sauce, sliced tomato, romaine lettuce or spinach leaves, plus slices of red onion

YOUR Morning and Afternoon Snack Choices

Fruit and Nuts

1/2 ounce raw nuts with an apple, banana, plum, pear, orange, wedge of melon, cup of berries, 2 kiwis, 1/2 grapefruit, or any other fruit

Grains and Berries

1/2 cup whole grain cereal mixed with 1/4 cup almonds and 1/4 cup dried berries, apricots, or raisins

Revved-up Veggies

1 cup of cut-up sautéed veggies, warmed in microwave and stuffed into small whole wheat pita

OR

Cut-up veggies dipped into 4 ounces plain, low-fat, no-sugar-added yogurt or low-fat cottage cheese mixed with lots of dill, chives, ginger, red pepper flakes, or other spices (your choice)

OR

Just plain cut-up veggies

Fruit and Yogurt

Low-fat probiotic (live culture) yogurt covered with 1/2 cup canned, unsweetened peaches or mandarin oranges and some raisins or Lifestyle 180 Vita-Mix Green Smoothie, with psyllium husks added (page 66)

YOUR Dessert Choices

Eat Every Other Day

Sliced Peaches with Raspberries, Blueberries, and Chocolate Chips (page 75)

OR

1 ounce of dark chocolate (made with real cocoa), approximately three or four bites

YOUR Dinner Choices

(But Don't Eat After 8:30 p.m.)

Stuffed Whole Wheat Pizza (page 73)

YOUR Drink Choices

Plain or sparkling water (with fruit slice if desired), skim milk, coffee, hot or iced tea (decaffeinated is best if you have problems sleeping), diet soda (but only 1 to 2 a day)

For breakfast, you may include an 8-ounce glass of fruit or vegetable juice, such as tomato juice or 100 percent grapefruit juice or orange juice with pulp, fortified with calcium and vitamin D

For dinner, you can include one glass of alcohol, which we prefer you to drink toward the end of the meal so it does not hinder your satiety center's ability to slow your voracious appetite. If you're a nondrinker, it's OK to swap for a teetotaler's cocktail made with low-sugar grape juice, sparkling water, and lime

DAY FIVE

YOUR Breakfast Choices

For Cereal Lovers

Cooked oat cereal with 4 ounces of skim milk, or soy milk fortified with vitamin D and calcium, and 1 fistful of your favorite fruit

OR

1 cup Kashi high-fiber or cold-oat cereal (like plain Cheerios) with 1 fistful of your favorite fruit, with 4 ounces of skim milk, or soy milk fortified with vitamin D and calcium

For Egg Lovers

Egg-white omelet (3 egg whites and 1 whole egg), plus cut-up mixed veggies

OR

2 scrambled, poached, or hard-boiled eggs with 2 pieces of lean turkey sausage or tofu sausage (scramble with a little canola Pam spray, not butter)

For Bread Lovers

1 slice toasted 100% whole wheat bread with 1 teaspoon peanut butter, or 1 teaspoon apple or walnut butter or avocado spread

For Breakfast Haters

Magical Breakfast Blaster (see recipe, page 63)

YOUR Lunch Choices

Meal-Size Salad

Chopped salad: 6 chopped walnuts, chopped veggies (your choice), and chopped mixed greens tossed with 4 ounces of salmon, turkey, or chicken breast; with balsamic vinegar (2 parts) and olive oil (1 part) dressing

Soup and Salad

1 cup of Garden Harvest Soup (page 67) or Lisa's Great Gazpacho (page 68) and small chopped salad with veggies or a non-

Caesar salad using olive or canola oil, or balsamic vinegar and olive oil dressing

Healthy Burger

Veggie burger or Boca Spicy Chik'n Patty on a toasted whole wheat English muffin with 1 tablespoon of fructose-free olive oil–based marinara sauce, sliced tomato, romaine lettuce or spinach leaves, plus slices of red onion

YOUR Morning and Afternoon Snack Choices

Fruit and Nuts

1/2 ounce raw nuts with an apple, banana, plum, pear, orange, wedge of melon, cup of berries, 2 kiwis, 1/2 grapefruit, or any other fruit

Grains and Berries

1/2 cup whole grain cereal mixed with 1/4 cup almonds and 1/4 cup dried berries, apricots, or raisins

Revved-up Veggies

1 cup of cut-up sautéed veggies, warmed in microwave and stuffed into small whole wheat pita

OR

Cut-up veggies dipped into 4 ounces plain, low-fat, no-sugar-added yogurt or low-fat cottage cheese mixed with lots of dill, chives, ginger, red pepper flakes, or other spices (your choice)

OR

Just plain cut-up veggies

Fruit and Yogurt

Low-fat probiotic (live culture) yogurt covered with 1/2 cup canned, unsweetened peaches or mandarin oranges and some raisins or Lifestyle 180 Vita-Mix Green Smoothie, with psyllium husks added (page 66)

YOUR Dessert Choices

Eat Every Other Day

Sliced Peaches with Raspberries, Blueberries, and Chocolate Chips (page 75)

OR

1 ounce of dark chocolate (made with real cocoa), approximately three or four bites

YOUR Dinner Choices

(But Don't Eat After 8:30 p.m.)

A small plate covered with vegetables (sautéed in olive oil), with lean protein like turkey, chicken, or salmon, with 100 percent whole-grain pasta or rice

YOUR Drink Choices

Plain or sparkling water (with fruit slice if desired), skim milk, coffee, hot or iced tea (decaffeinated is best if you have problems sleeping), diet soda (but only 1 to 2 a day)

For breakfast, you may include an 8-ounce

glass of fruit or vegetable juice, such as tomato juice or 100 percent grapefruit juice or orange juice with pulp, fortified with calcium and vitamin D

For dinner, you can include one glass of alcohol, which we prefer you to drink toward the end of the meal so it does not hinder your satiety center's ability to slow your voracious appetite. If you're a nondrinker, it's OK to swap for a teetotaler's cocktail made with low-sugar grape juice, sparkling water, and lime

DAY SIX

YOUR Breakfast Choices

For Cereal Lovers

Cooked oat cereal with 4 ounces of skim milk, or soy milk fortified with vitamin D and calcium, and 1 fistful of your favorite fruit

OR

1 cup Kashi high-fiber or cold-oat cereal

(like plain Cheerios) with 1 fistful of your favorite fruit, with 4 ounces of skim milk, or soy milk fortified with vitamin D and calcium

For Egg Lovers

Egg-white omelet (3 egg whites and 1 whole egg), plus cut-up mixed veggies

OR

2 scrambled, poached, or hard-boiled eggs with 2 pieces of lean turkey sausage or tofu sausage (scramble with a little canola Pam spray, not butter)

For Bread Lovers

1 slice toasted 100% whole wheat bread with 1 teaspoon peanut butter, or 1 teaspoon apple or walnut butter or avocado spread

For Breakfast Haters

Magical Breakfast Blaster (see recipe, page 63)

YOUR Lunch Choices

Meal-Size Salad

Chopped salad: 6 chopped walnuts, chopped veggies (your choice), and chopped mixed greens tossed with 4 ounces of salmon, turkey, or chicken breast; with balsamic vinegar (2 parts) and olive oil (1 part) dressing

Soup and Salad

1 cup of Garden Harvest Soup (page 67) or Lisa's Great Gazpacho (page 68) and small chopped salad with veggies or a non-Caesar salad using olive or canola oil, or balsamic vinegar and olive oil dressing

Healthy Burger

Veggie burger or Boca Spicy Chik'n Patty on a toasted whole wheat English muffin with 1 tablespoon of fructose-free olive oil–based marinara sauce, sliced tomato, romaine lettuce or spinach leaves, plus slices of red onion

YOUR Morning and Afternoon Snack Choices

Fruit and Nuts

1/2 ounce raw nuts with an apple, banana, plum, pear, orange, wedge of melon, cup of berries, 2 kiwis, 1/2 grapefruit, or any other fruit

Grains and Berries

1/2 cup whole grain cereal mixed with 1/4 cup almonds and 1/4 cup dried berries, apricots, or raisins

Revved-up Veggies

1 cup of cut-up sautéed veggies, warmed in microwave and stuffed into small whole wheat pita

OR

Cut-up veggies dipped into 4 ounces plain, low-fat, no-sugar-added yogurt or low-fat cottage cheese mixed with lots of dill, chives, ginger, red pepper flakes, or other spices (your choice)

OR

Just plain cut-up veggies

Fruit and Yogurt

Low-fat probiotic (live culture) yogurt
covered with 1/2 cup canned, unsweetened
peaches or mandarin oranges and some
raisins or Lifestyle 180 Vita-Mix Green
Smoothie, with psyllium husks added (page
66)

YOUR Dessert Choices

Eat Every Other Day

Sliced Peaches with Raspberries,
Blueberries, and Chocolate Chips (page 75)

OR

1 ounce of dark chocolate (made with real
cocoa), approximately three or four bites

YOUR Dinner Choices

BONUS RECIPE!

Lifestyle 180 Chia Sausage or Meatballs

12 servings ❖ 130 calories per serving

3/4 cup nonalcoholic red wine
2 tablespoons finely minced garlic
2 tablespoons ground chia seeds
1 tablespoon fennel seed
1/2 teaspoon dried basil
1/4 teaspoon dried oregano
1/4 teaspoon dried thyme
1/4 teaspoon freshly ground black pepper
2 teaspoons seasoned salt
1/2 teaspoon crushed red pepper flakes
1/4 cup chopped fresh parsley
2 pounds ground turkey breast

In large bowl combine nonalcoholic red wine, garlic, and chia seeds. Set aside and allow chia seeds to swell for 30 minutes.

Add remaining ingredients except for turkey and mix well. Add turkey and mix until well blended. In a large nonstick pan, cook sausage in either patty form or bulk form until slightly brown and stir to crumble. Drain and serve or cool and refrigerate.

YOUR Drink Choices

Plain or sparkling water (with fruit slice if desired), skim milk, coffee, hot or iced tea (decaffeinated is best if you have problems sleeping), diet soda (but only 1 to 2 a day)

For breakfast, you may include an 8-ounce glass of fruit or vegetable juice, such as tomato juice or 100 percent grapefruit juice or orange juice with pulp, fortified with calcium and vitamin D

For dinner, you can include one glass of alcohol, which we prefer you to drink toward the end of the meal so it does not hinder your satiety center's ability to slow your voracious appetite. If you're a nondrinker, it's OK to swap for a teetotaler's cocktail made with low-sugar grape juice, sparkling water, and lime

DAY SEVEN

YOUR Breakfast Choices

For Cereal Lovers

Cooked oat cereal with 4 ounces of skim milk, or soy milk fortified with vitamin D and calcium, and 1 fistful of your favorite fruit

OR

1 cup Kashi high-fiber or cold-oat cereal (like plain Cheerios) with 1 fistful of your favorite fruit, with 4 ounces of skim milk, or soy milk fortified with vitamin D and calcium

For Egg Lovers

Egg-white omelet (3 egg whites and 1 whole egg), plus cut-up mixed veggies

OR

2 scrambled, poached, or hard-boiled eggs with 2 pieces of lean turkey sausage or tofu

sausage (scramble with a little canola Pam spray, not butter)

For Bread Lovers

1 slice toasted 100% whole wheat bread with 1 teaspoon peanut butter, or 1 teaspoon apple or walnut butter or avocado spread

For Breakfast Haters

Magical Breakfast Blaster (see recipe, page 63)

YOUR Lunch Choices

Meal-Size Salad

Chopped salad: 6 chopped walnuts, chopped veggies (your choice), and chopped mixed greens tossed with 4 ounces of salmon, turkey, or chicken breast; with balsamic vinegar (2 parts) and olive oil (1 part) dressing

Soup and Salad

1 cup of Garden Harvest Soup (page 67)

or Lisa's Great Gazpacho (page 68) and small chopped salad with veggies or a non-Caesar salad using olive or canola oil, or balsamic vinegar and olive oil dressing

Healthy Burger

Veggie burger or Boca Spicy Chik'n Patty on a toasted whole wheat English muffin with 1 tablespoon of fructose-free olive oil–based marinara sauce, sliced tomato, romaine lettuce or spinach leaves, plus slices of red onion

YOUR Morning and Afternoon Snack Choices

Fruit and Nuts

1/2 ounce raw nuts with an apple, banana, plum, pear, orange, wedge of melon, cup of berries, 2 kiwis, 1/2 grapefruit, or any other fruit

Grains and Berries

1/2 cup whole grain cereal mixed with 1/4 cup almonds and 1/4 cup dried berries, apricots, or raisins

Revved-up Veggies

1 cup of cut-up sautéed veggies, warmed in microwave and stuffed into small whole wheat pita

OR

Cut-up veggies dipped into 4 ounces plain, low-fat, no-sugar-added yogurt or low-fat cottage cheese mixed with lots of dill, chives, ginger, red pepper flakes, or other spices (your choice)

OR

Just plain cut-up veggies

Fruit and Yogurt

Low-fat probiotic (live culture) yogurt covered with 1/2 cup canned, unsweetened peaches or mandarin oranges and some raisins or Lifestyle 180 Vita-Mix Green Smoothie, with psyllium husks added (page 66)

YOUR Dessert Choices

Sliced Peaches with Raspberries, Blueberries, and Chocolate Chips (page 75)

OR

1 ounce of dark chocolate (made with real cocoa), approximately three or four bites

YOUR Dinner Choices

BONUS RECIPE!

Pork Tenderloin with Broccoli and Szechuan Noodles
6 servings (1 cup each) ❖ 330 calories per serving

Szechuan Noodles

1 pound 100 percent whole wheat spaghetti

3 1/2 tablespoons dark toasted sesame oil

3 1/2 tablespoons soy sauce

1 1/2 tablespoons balsamic vinegar
2 teaspoons agave nectar
1 tablespoon hot chile toasted sesame oil
1/2 teaspoon finely chopped garlic
1/3 cup sliced scallions

Cook spaghetti as directed on package, drain, and rinse to cool. In a separate bowl, combine the other ingredients and mix well. Toss with spaghetti, cover, and refrigerate.

Broccoli
3 cups broccoli florets

Add water to a large pot and bring to boil. Lightly salt the water and add broccoli florets and blanch for about 3 minutes or until just tender. Remove broccoli with slotted spoon, drain well, place on a flat baking tray, and allow to cool.

Pork Tenderloin
3 tablespoons agave nectar
1 tablespoon balsamic vinegar

1 tablespoon tamari sauce
1 teaspoon grated fresh ginger
1 teaspoon finely minced garlic
2 tablespoons rice wine vinegar
12 ounces pork tenderloin cut into two
  6-ounce pieces

Combine agave nectar, balsamic vinegar, tamari sauce, ginger, garlic, and rice wine vinegar in a bowl and marinate pork in the refrigerator for 30 minutes. Set pork tenderloin on rimmed baking sheet and preheat oven to 375°F. Add marinade to small saucepan and bring to a simmer. Cook until reduced by half (3 tablespoons) and allow to cool 5 minutes to a glaze consistency. Coat pork tenderloin with marinade glaze and roast in oven for about 25 minutes or until an instant read thermometer inserted in the thickest part reads 150°F internal temperature. Allow to rest 10 minutes, slice into six 2-ounce pieces, and serve each piece with 1/2 cup broccoli and 1/2 cup Szechuan noodles.

YOUR Drink Choices

Plain or sparkling water (with fruit slice if desired), skim milk, coffee, hot or iced tea (decaffeinated is best if you have problems sleeping), diet soda (but only 1 to 2 a day)

For breakfast, you may include an 8-ounce glass of fruit or vegetable juice, such as tomato juice or 100 percent grapefruit juice or orange juice with pulp, fortified with calcium and vitamin D

For dinner, you can include one glass of alcohol, which we prefer you to drink toward the end of the meal so it does not hinder your satiety center's ability to slow your voracious appetite. If you're a nondrinker, it's OK to swap for a teetotaler's cocktail made with low-sugar grape juice, sparkling water, and lime

Days 8 through 14

Repeat Days 1 through 7.

ABOUT THE AUTHORS

Michael F. Roizen, MD, is a *New York Times* bestselling author and cofounder and originator of the very popular RealAge.com website. He is chief wellness officer of the Cleveland Clinic, chair of its Wellness Institute, and chief medical consultant to *The Dr. Oz Show* and chief medical expert for AOL Health.

Mehmet C. Oz, MD, is also a *New York Times* bestselling author and the Emmy Award–winning host of *The Dr. Oz Show*. He is professor and vice chairman of surgery at New York Presbyterian Columbia University and the medical director of the Integrated Medicine Center and the director of the Heart Institute.